Background

I0489186

In April 2012, the Treasury Inspector General for Tax Administration received an allegation about an August 2010 Internal Revenue Service (IRS) conference held in Anaheim, California, (hereafter referred to as the Anaheim conference or the conference) that may have involved excessive spending. The Small Business/Self-Employed (SB/SE) Division held the conference, entitled "Leading into the Future," for its entire management staff. According to information provided by the IRS, this conference was provided to 2,609 employees at an estimated cost of approximately $4.1 million.

We requested a complete list of conferences[1] held by the IRS during Fiscal Years (FY) 2010 through 2012. Based on information provided to us, the IRS held 225 conferences during this period for a total estimated cost of approximately $49 million. See Appendices IV and VI for more information on these conferences. Figure 1 shows the top three conferences held at a single location, based on estimated cost per the IRS.

Figure 1: Top Three Conferences Based on Estimated Cost Held at a Single Location During FYs 2010 Through 2012

Operating Division	Name/Purpose of Event	Date	Location	Participants	Estimated Cost
SB/SE	SB/SE Division All Managers Continuing Professional Education (CPE)	August 2010	Anaheim, California	2,609	$4,133,183
Taxpayer Advocate Service (TAS)	TAS Technical Training Symposium	August 2010	Philadelphia, Pennsylvania	2,113	$2,933,042
SB/SE	SB/SE Division Collection Leadership CPE	March 2010	San Diego, California	721	$1,198,397

Source: Chief Financial Officer, November 2012.[2]

---

[1] For this audit, we defined conferences as an IRS-sponsored meeting, retreat, seminar, symposium, training, or other event that involved travel for 50 or more attendees. In addition, a conference is defined in the Federal Travel Regulations as, "...[a] meeting, retreat, seminar, symposium or event that involves attendee travel. The term 'conference' also applies to training activities that are considered to be conferences under 5 CFR 410.404." See 41 CFR 300-3.1.

[2] The Treasury Inspector General for Tax Administration has only reviewed the SB/SE Division Leadership Conference described in this report and has not performed any detailed analysis of the other conferences held during FYs 2010 through 2012. Although we obtained a list of 225 conferences, we focused on the Anaheim conference based on an allegation received.

As a result of the allegation related to the August 2010 Anaheim conference and the fact that it was the most expensive conference reported by the IRS during FYs 2010 through 2012, we focused our audit work on assessing the IRS's spending related to this conference.

In the current economic environment, Congress and the President have focused on ways to reduce unnecessary, inefficient, and wasteful spending. In June 2011, the President launched a Governmentwide "Campaign to Cut Waste" to target ineffective and wasteful spending. On November 9, 2011, the President signed Executive Order 13589, *Promoting Efficient Spending*, reinforcing the Administration's commitment to cutting waste in Federal Government spending and identifying opportunities to promote efficient and effective spending. As part of this Executive Order, agencies were directed to make all appropriate efforts to conduct business and host or sponsor conferences in space controlled by the Federal Government, wherever practicable and cost effective. Excessive spending by Federal agencies on management conferences has been highlighted by recent Inspectors General reports[3] and has been the subject of congressional hearings.

Beginning in February 2011, the IRS issued a number of policy guidance documents to minimize spending on travel and conferences. This guidance related to eliminating all face-to-face managers' meetings unless approved by the Deputy Commissioners as well as limiting training to only mission-critical technical training delivered remotely whenever possible (February 2011); discontinuing the purchase of promotional items unless approved by the Deputy Commissioners (August 2011); further reducing all travel and training by 10 percent (November 2011); and establishing new procedures requiring Deputy Commissioner approval of conference-related activities (December 2011). On March 2, 2012, the IRS Chief Financial Officer issued consolidated guidance for events hosted by the IRS including, but not limited to, conferences, training, and meetings. The guidance includes pertinent information on approvals, event planning, refreshments, site selection, procurement, promotional items, and recordkeeping requirements.

In May 2012, the Office of Management and Budget[4] issued guidelines which stipulate that agencies may not incur net expenses greater than $500,000 for a single conference and agencies must publicly report (on their official website) all conference expenses in excess of $100,000. Department of the Treasury guidance implemented in November 2012 further requires that any conference hosted or sponsored by Department of the Treasury bureaus costing $250,000 or more be approved by the Treasury Secretary, and that those requiring the use of event planners

---

[3] U.S. General Services Administration Office of Inspector General, *Management Deficiency Report: General Services Administration Public Buildings Service 2010 Western Regions Conference* (Apr. 2, 2012), and Veterans Administration Office of Inspector General, *Department of Veterans Affairs Administrative Investigation of the FY 2011 Human Resources Conferences in Orlando, Florida* (Sept. 30, 2012).

[4] Office of Management and Budget, Memorandum M12-12, *Promoting Efficient Spending to Support Agency Operations* (May 2012).

(for assistance in site selection) be approved in advance by the Department of the Treasury's Office of the Assistant Secretary for Management and Chief Financial Officer.

This review was performed in coordination with the Chief Financial Office of Internal Control and SB/SE Division's Strategy and Finance office in Washington, D.C., during the period October 2012 through March 2013. We conducted this performance audit in accordance with generally accepted government auditing standards. Those standards require that we plan and perform the audit to obtain sufficient, appropriate evidence to provide a reasonable basis for our findings and conclusions based on our audit objective. We believe that the evidence obtained provides a reasonable basis for our findings and conclusions based on our audit objective. We did not evaluate the appropriateness or relevance of the training provided at the Anaheim conference. It was beyond the scope of this review to assess the merits and effectiveness of the conference agenda. Detailed information on our audit objective, scope, and methodology is presented in Appendix I. Major contributors to the report are listed in Appendix II.

Results of Review

The Anaheim Conference Was Approved by Both Internal Revenue Service Deputy Commissioners

SB/SE Division management requested and received approval for the Anaheim conference as required based on IRS procedures in place at that time. Specifically, we determined that the Deputy Commissioners, Operations Support and Services and Enforcement, both approved the request for the Anaheim conference on April 12, 2010. At the time of approval, the estimated cost was approximately $4.3 million. The request approved by the Deputy Commissioners was for a "Small Business/Self-Employed All Managers CPE;" however, SB/SE Division management informed us that no CPE credits were provided to any attendees for the specific conference sessions. IRS management stated that all attendees were credited with 24 hours of leadership training that was recorded in the IRS's training system. However, SB/SE Division management also stated that attendees were not required to document their attendance at any conference session.

Procedures at that time required Deputy Commissioner approval for any conference exceeding an estimated cost of $100,000. In December 2011, the IRS issued guidance for events hosted by the IRS including, but not limited to, conferences, training, and meetings. The guidance includes pertinent information on approvals, event planning, refreshments, site selection, procurement, promotional items, and recordkeeping requirements. These procedures now require Deputy Commissioner approval for any event that meets or exceeds a $20,000 threshold; any event involving the purchase of light refreshments, food, or mementos; or any event held at non-Government facilities. In addition, in May 2012, the Office of Management and Budget issued new guidelines which stipulate that agencies may not incur net expenses greater than $500,000 for a single conference and that agencies must publicly report (on their official website) all conference expenses in excess of $100,000. Department of the Treasury guidance implemented in November 2012 now requires any conference hosted or sponsored by Department of the Treasury bureaus costing $250,000 or more be approved by the Treasury Secretary.

Conference Costs Were Primarily Paid Through Unused Funding Originally Intended for Hiring Enforcement Employees

According to SB/SE Division management, the SB/SE Division was allocated $132.7 million in the IRS's FY 2010 budget to hire 1,315 full-time employees. SB/SE Division management stated that the resources were provided for several initiatives, such as improving the reporting compliance of taxpayers, addressing nonfiling/underpayment and collection coverage, reducing the Tax Gap[5] attributable to globalization, and expanding document matching for small business taxpayers. IRS management stated the $132.7 million enforcement hiring funds were provided for both salary and training of any new hires and indicated that approximately $18 million of this funding was available for training purposes.

According to SB/SE Division management, 1,516 hires were made during FY 2010. The majority of these were front-line positions such as revenue officers, revenue agents, and tax compliance officers. However, because the new hires were not on board for the full year, IRS management stated that there were unused funds obtained for the hiring initiative that would have lapsed at the end of FY 2010.

SB/SE Division management transferred $3.2 million from the hiring initiative to help fund the conference. They also indicated that they used training funds to cover the additional conference expenses. SB/SE Division management indicated that IRS business units have the authority to reprogram funds to meet their program needs. We did not identify any restrictions preventing the IRS from using these available funds to pay for the conference.

Conference Costs Were Not Adequately Tracked and Monitored

When initially requesting the approval of the Deputy Commissioners, SB/SE Division management estimated the Anaheim conference's total cost as $4,297,285. As shown in Appendix VII, the IRS indicated that the final cost for the conference was $4,133,183.

While IRS management provided documentation showing the total final costs at $4.1 million, we could not obtain reasonable assurance that this amount represents a full and accurate accounting of the conference costs. The IRS was unable to provide documentation to support all costs associated with the conference. Although IRS management established an internal tracking code for employees to charge their conference travel, we determined that this code was not always used as required. For example, we identified 188 employees who attended the conference but did not use the code on their travel voucher (representing approximately $245,000). As a result, we cannot validate that the "final" conference cost of $4.1 million reported by the IRS and detailed in Appendix VII is accurate.

In addition, we requested supporting documentation related to the $50,187 expended for "videos." However, IRS management stated that this was an estimated cost and could not provide detail on how this cost was estimated. In addition, IRS management could not provide any supporting documentation detailing how this money was spent.

---

[5] The Tax Gap is the estimated difference between the amount of tax that taxpayers should pay and the amount that is paid voluntarily and on time.

Further, IRS management originally estimated that 2,609 employees were expected to attend the conference. SB/SE Division management stated that the cost for all employee travel was $3,752,000.[6] However, we reviewed travel voucher documentation and identified that 2,547 vouchers were filed by IRS employees claiming approximately $3,845,000 associated with the conference.

At the time the Anaheim conference was planned and conducted, the IRS did not have any guidelines requiring management to track and report the actual costs incurred for conferences. In March 2012, the IRS Chief Financial Officer issued a memorandum establishing additional controls for event-related spending. This guidance now requires each office conducting a conference to establish a methodology to identify, track, and review various conference events, including costs associated with planning and attending the conference. In addition, each office is required to maintain documentation related to conference planning and attendance to allow for subsequent audit review and management inquiry.

We did not assess whether these new requirements have been implemented and are operating effectively to track actual costs related to conferences held after the March 2012 memorandum was issued. However, we believe IRS management should verify that adequate information is now being tracked and maintained by offices to accurately account for actual conference costs.

Recommendations

The Chief Financial Officer should:

Recommendation 1: For conferences held after issuance of the March 2012 procedures, verify that appropriate information is being tracked and maintained by IRS offices to accurately account for actual conference costs and attendance.

> **Management's Response:** The IRS agreed with this recommendation. The Chief Financial Officer will update the December 27, 2012, Interim Guidance Memorandum, *Reissued Interim Guidance on the Approval Process for Event-Related Spending*, to include a requirement for the Chief Financial Officer to review, on a rotating basis, documentation maintained by the business units for conference and event-related spending.

Recommendation 2: Implement a policy to determine whether specific sessions at conferences qualify for CPE credits.

> **Management's Response:** The IRS agreed with this recommendation. The IRS Human Capital Office will strengthen the policy and guidance for determining when a course may be eligible for Certified Public Accountant CPE certification credit in Internal

---

[6] This total excludes travel for planning trips conducted prior to the conference.

Revenue Manual (IRM) 6.410.1.3.3.3, *Credit for Continuing Professional Education for Certified Public Accountants.*

The Process Used to Select Anaheim As the Conference Site Did Not Follow Established Guidelines

The process followed by IRS management to identify Anaheim as the conference location did not follow established procedures and may not have resulted in the most cost-effective site being identified for the conference. Specifically, IRS management did not use available internal personnel to assist in searching for the most cost-effective location as required. According to the IRS, SB/SE Division management gave six employees awards totaling $6,000 for their work on the Anaheim conference, including two employees who each received $2,000 who were primarily responsible for coordinating the conference planning.

IRS personnel responsible for identifying conference space were not used

Within the IRS, the Centralized Delivery Services (CDS) function was established to assist IRS management in planning training events. The CDS function is responsible for coordinating conference space for IRS events, including locating off-site training space. The CDS function works with the Office of Procurement to identify the most cost-effective off-site facilities when needed. CDS function personnel are responsible for researching at least three alternate off-site facilities and preparing a cost comparison.

However, SB/SE Division management did not use CDS function personnel to select Anaheim as the conference location. Instead, they relied on non-governmental event planners who were not under contract with the IRS and who were selected based on past relationships with the IRS to identify possible off-site locations. SB/SE Division management stated that their business practice was to complete their own research for all conferences, including the preparation of all cost comparisons and required forms.

IRS guidelines require that Government facilities must be used for training activities, meetings, and conferences when available and adequate to meet training objectives. Non-Government facilities should be used only when Government space is not available or Government space does not meet training requirements due to special circumstances. IRS guidelines indicate that non-Government facilities should be avoided except where it can be demonstrated that the anticipated benefits will more than offset any additional direct expenditures and will not give the general public an appearance of unnecessary spending by the IRS.

When off-site facilities are used, CDS function personnel are required to provide documentation that establishes that Government property was considered but was determined not available and explains why any available Government space does not meet the business needs of the conference. Although the CDS function was not used in the site selection process,

SB/SE Division management stated that they believed that SB/SE Division personnel prepared this documentation. However, they were unable to locate the documentation.

Letters of Intent are used by the IRS to state the IRS's intent to hold off-site training at hotels and secure the hotels' cooperation in reserving space until funding has been approved. Although CDS or Procurement function personnel are normally required to sign Letters of Intent, a General Schedule-14 SB/SE Division revenue officer in charge of conference planning signed the Letters of Intent with the three hotels.[7] The Letters of Intent detailed the potential number of rooms to be blocked by the hotels as well as the services the hotels agreed to provide in exchange for the IRS's business. These services included continental breakfast each day for all attendees, a welcome reception with two drink coupons for all attendees, and room upgrades. In addition, the Letters of Intent stated that the three hotels would pay a 5 percent commission to each of the two event planners based on the number of rooms and lodging rate paid by the IRS.

Non-governmental event planners representing the IRS were not under contract and were paid $133,000 by the conference hotels

Instead of using the required IRS personnel, SB/SE Division management contacted two non-governmental event planners to identify a suitable off-site location for the conference. SB/SE Division management stated that these two event planners were selected based on prior work performed for the IRS. Although operating on behalf of the IRS, the IRS had no contractual agreement with these two individuals. IRS procedures currently require background investigations and tax compliance checks be performed on contractors doing business with the IRS. However, because the IRS had no contractual agreement with these event planners, the IRS did not perform background or tax compliance checks on these two individuals.

Despite having no contractual agreement with the IRS, these event planners were responsible for issuing Requests for Proposals to hotels and receiving the hotel responses (one event planner was responsible for the eastern part of the United States and the other for the western part of the United States). SB/SE Division management advised us that the Requests for Proposals were analyzed by the event planners and SB/SE Division personnel.

Based on review of the responses received from the Requests for Proposals, IRS management informed us that three possible locations for the conference were identified: Anaheim, California; San Francisco, California; and Dallas, Texas. However, no documentation was available that details how these three locations were ultimately identified from the responses received. Ultimately, Anaheim was selected for the conference.

SB/SE Division management did not enter into a signed contract with the two event planners nor did they directly pay them for their services. Instead, the event planners were each paid a 5 percent commission directly by the hotels based on the number of rooms used by the IRS for

---

[7] The revenue officer mentioned in this section is the same revenue officer mentioned in other sections of the report.

the conference. Based on information provided by SB/SE Division management, we estimate the event planners were paid approximately $133,000 by the hotels (or approximately $66,500 each).

The use of the planners in this process increased the possibility that the site selection did not result in the lowest cost to the Government. For example, the event planners had no incentive to negotiate a lower Government room rate at any conference location because they were directly compensated based on the room rate. In addition, the IRS received additional services at the conference, such as continental breakfast each day for all attendees, a welcome reception with two drink coupons for all attendees, room upgrades, free Internet, and free meeting space. The IRS was unable to provide us with any documentation detailing any negotiations conducted with the hotels related to the conference expenses. We question whether the room rate could have been negotiated at a lower rate if some of these services were not included and event planners were not used. The hotels' willingness to pay a commission to the planners indicates that additional room discounts may have been available to the IRS. An IRS Procurement Officer advised us that the IRS has previously been able to negotiate lower room rates, below per diem,[8] when a large number of rooms were reserved at one time. In addition, a national sales representative for Hilton Hotels and Resorts stated that they would negotiate room rates lower than the Government per diem depending on the number of rooms, location, and time of year.

We did not identify any policy or guidance in place at the time the conference was conducted outlining the appropriate use of non-governmental event planners and how these types of individuals should be selected for use by IRS management. Department of the Treasury guidance[9] implemented in November 2012 places limitations on the use of planners because their use can reduce the Department of the Treasury's control over conference expenses and can increase costs. This guidance now requires the Department of the Treasury's Office of the Assistant Secretary for Management and Chief Financial Officer to approve in advance the use of event planners for conference site selection.

Recommendations

The Chief Financial Officer should:

Recommendation 3: Reemphasize existing procedures to ensure that business units contact CDS function personnel to coordinate planning of any future conference or event. Further, additional procedures should be developed that require all documentation supporting the selection of non-Government facilities for future conferences be maintained for management review.

---

[8] The per diem allowance (also referred to as subsistence allowance) is a daily payment instead of reimbursement for actual expenses for lodging, meals, and related incidental expenses.
[9] Treasury Directive 12-70, *Hosted or Sponsored Conference Planning and Approval*, November 28, 2012.

Management's Response: The IRS agreed with this recommendation. The Agency-Wide Shared Services Procurement office will update and reissue Policy and Procedures Memorandum No. 70.24, *Acquiring Training, Meeting and Conference Space*, to reflect guidance in Treasury Directive 12-70 and reemphasize existing procedures for planning conferences or events and maintaining supporting documentation. The Human Capital Office will update IRM 6.410.1, *Leadership and Education, Selection of Off-Site Locations and Facilities for Training*, to include procedures that require all documentation supporting the selection of non-Government facilities for future conferences be maintained for management review.

Recommendation 4: Develop and implement procedures outlining the appropriate use of non-governmental event planners when planning IRS conferences. This should include how event planners are selected and compensated.

Management's Response: The IRS agreed with this recommendation. The Chief Financial Officer issued the December 27, 2012, Interim Guidance Memorandum, *Reissued Interim Guidance on the Approval Process for Event-Related Spending,* which limits the use of external event planners. The Human Capital Office will update IRM 6.410.1, *Leadership and Education, Selection of Off-Site Locations and Facilities for Training,* to include guidance on the use, selection, and compensation of event planners for those instances in which event planners must be used.

Planning Trips Were Made for the Conference

IRS employees made the following planning trips before the conference was held:

- A November 2009 planning trip by three IRS employees and the two event planners to Anaheim, California, and San Francisco, California, to review potential hotels for the conference. SB/SE Division management stated that these hotels had responded to the event planners' Requests for Proposals as a potential conference site and that the visits were made to inspect the location, space, and audiovisual technology to determine which site best met the meeting requirements. The cost of the IRS employees' travel for this trip was approximately $3,500.

- A June 2010 planning trip by eight IRS employees to Anaheim, California, at a cost of approximately $10,300. IRS management stated that this trip was performed to meet with the sales, convention services, audiovisual, reservations, and catering staff from each hotel to discuss various issues, including room commitment, reservations, cancellation fees, number of rooms required for conference attendees with disabilities, shipping and receiving, and storage. In addition, IRS management stated that internal discussions with IRS personnel were held to discuss staffing and support needs.

- An August 2010 (the week before the conference was held) planning trip to Anaheim, California, by 16 IRS employees at a cost of approximately $22,000. SB/SE Division management does not consider this a "planning" trip and stated that support personnel traveled to Anaheim the week prior to the conference to handle all setup work.

We did not identify any policy or guidance that outlined the reason(s) when and why planning trips should be performed for conferences, the appropriate number of employees necessary for these types of trips, and whether a senior management official should approve these trips in advance. However, the costs associated with these planning trips may have been excessive based on the number of employees who were involved. Although some local employees were involved in planning for the conference, additional local SB/SE Division employees who attended the conference may have been able to perform more of the planning steps to reduce further the overall costs.

Recommendation

Recommendation 5: The Chief Financial Officer should establish procedures clearly outlining when planning trips should be performed for conferences. These procedures should require documentation of the reason and estimated cost for planning trips, along with the requirement that local IRS employees are used to the extent possible to perform these planning trips. This information should be provided to a designated management official or an executive for approval.

> **Management's Response:** The IRS agreed with this recommendation. The Human Capital Office will update IRM 6.410.1 *Leadership and Education, Selection of Off-Site Locations and Facilities for Training,* to emphasize the requirement to document the reason for and estimated cost of planning trips and to maintain documentation of executive approval of the planning trip.

Fifteen Outside Speakers Were Contracted for the Conference

For the conference, SB/SE Division management contracted with 15 outside speakers for presentations at a total cost of $135,350.[10] For 13 of these speakers, SB/SE Division management used sole-source contracts specifically requesting the speakers used.[11] A sole-source contract is used when a determination is made that only one individual or company can perform the requested service. These contracts all related to leadership topics. The same

---

[10] See Appendix VIII for a list of the speakers and a description of the services provided.
[11] Services for the remaining two speakers (Mark Nishan and Vincent Stovall) were obtained using a Standard Form 182, *Request, Authorization, Agreement & Certification of Training.* SB/SE Division management stated that these two speakers were identified later in the conference planning, and they did not have ample time to use the sole-source process.

General Schedule-14 revenue officer previously discussed who was in charge of planning the conference prepared and signed the sole-source justification on behalf of SB/SE Division management. SB/SE Division management stated that the process for selecting the 15 outside speakers included a committee of SB/SE Division senior management who made the decision regarding speaker topics and identified potential speakers. According to IRS management, the committee presented the agenda, workshops, and keynote speakers to the SB/SE Division Commissioner, who ultimately approved them.

The conference featured 15 speakers at a cost of $135,350

The IRS paid for 15 outside speakers and offered additional workshops conducted by IRS management. Appendix X shows that 24 workshops ("knowledge portals") were presented on the second day of the conference (10 workshops conducted by IRS speakers and 14 workshops presented by external speakers paid by the IRS). These workshops were conducted multiple times (generally four times by each speaker) during this day. As a result, attendees could choose from between 22 to 23 different workshops at each of the four workshop session times that could be attended. Because 10 of these workshops were conducted by IRS personnel, some attendees may not have viewed any of the workshops conducted by the paid external speakers.

Two keynote speakers were featured

In addition to the 24 workshops presented on the second day of the conference, the IRS paid two additional speakers to present keynote addresses at the conference. One keynote speaker presented the same speech for two sessions on the first day of the conference. The second keynote speaker presented his keynote address for two sessions on the last day of the conference. Based on the conference agenda, all attendees had the opportunity to attend both keynote speeches.

One keynote speaker was contracted to perform two keynote speeches that lasted approximately one hour each, and the speaker was paid $17,000. According to the contract signed by the IRS, this speaker was "uniquely qualified to deliver this presentation because of the combination of his artistic abilities and his presentation skills. In each presentation, he will create a unique painting that reinforces his message of unlearning the rules, breaking the boundaries, and freeing the thought process to find creative solutions to challenges."

The speaker created six paintings at these two keynote sessions (three at each session). These paintings consisted of the following portraits: Albert Einstein (one); Michael Jordan (one); Abraham Lincoln (one); U2 singer Bono (one); and the Statute of Liberty (two).

At each session, one attendee was selected by the speaker and presented with one of the paintings. SB/SE Division management indicated that three paintings were donated to the

Combined Federal Campaign[12] as auction items (these paintings were sold for $75, $130, and $380). SB/SE Division management stated that the final painting prepared during these presentations was lost. Figure 2 shows an example of a painting prepared during the conference.

Figure 2: One of Six Paintings Created During the Keynote Presentation

Photo Removed Due to Copyright Restrictions

Source: Recorded conference sessions.

The second keynote speaker was paid $27,500 (including travel expenses) for two speeches lasting approximately one hour each. According to the contract signed by the IRS, this speaker was uniquely qualified because the presentation was based on a book published by the speaker, and the speaker "will share how seemingly random combinations of ideas can drive radical innovations. His concept of Intersectional Ideas illustrates how ideas from different fields can be combined to generate new solutions to existing challenges."

---

[12] The Combined Federal Campaign is a charity campaign created and run by Federal workers that raises funds to benefit authorized charities.

According to the contract, this speaker's fee of $27,500 included a $2,500 flat fee for travel, which the contracting officer authorized to accommodate first-class travel. According to the contracting officer, this travel charge was non-negotiable and was necessary in order to obtain the speaker. In addition, SB/SE Division management stated that the travel costs for "this top rated keynote speaker was appropriate." No travel receipts were obtained by the IRS for our review, and the contracting officer did not know whether the speaker traveled first class or not. We reviewed the speaker's fee schedule and determined that the speaker requires the payment of first-class airfare to domestic locations in addition to his speaking fee.

Star Trek Parody and "SB/SE Shuffle" Videos Were Produced for the Conference

As previously stated, the IRS reported that it expended $50,187 on "videos" for the conference, but was unable to provide any details supporting this cost. We determined that SB/SE Division management showed several videos at the conference, including a Star Trek parody and another video entitled "SB/SE Shuffle."

The conference theme was "Leading into the Future," with a Star Trek parody video shown at the beginning of the conference. This video consisted of a scripted presentation featuring SB/SE Division executives portraying Star Trek characters in a tax-themed parody. SB/SE Division management stated that the purpose of the video was to open the conference by highlighting "current issues facing the IRS and SB/SE [Division] in the leadership arena and set the stage for the many topics being covered at the conference." According to SB/SE Division management, the SB/SE Division Commissioner verbally approved the creation of the video.

Although SB/SE Division management did not track a specific cost associated with producing the Star Trek video, we determined the following:

- The Star Trek video was approximately 5 minutes and 40 seconds long and featured SB/SE Division executives in Star Trek costumes on a mock set of the Starship Enterprise. Per the SB/SE Division, employees purchased the costumes using personal funds.

- The IRS constructed a mock set at its television studio located in New Carrollton, Maryland, at a cost of $2,400. However, SB/SE Division management does not have any documentation supporting this amount.

- IRS personnel located at its New Carrollton television studio worked on the video production. The average grade for these IRS employees was a General Schedule-14.

- The SB/SE Division estimated that it takes 11 hours of staff work to produce one minute of finished video. Based on the length of the Star Trek video, we estimate it took approximately 62 staff hours to produce the final video. At a minimum hourly rate of

$50.00 for a General Schedule-14 employee, this converts to approximately $3,100 in staff time.

- No documentation was maintained to track any costs associated with the development of the other production costs, such as the script development, makeup, lighting, and videotaping.

In addition, a video entitled "SB/SE Shuffle" was produced featuring 15 SB/SE Division executives and managers dancing on a stage. This video was 2 minutes and 52 seconds long. This video was shown during the conference and "was designed to engage managers and help facilitate a connection between executives and managers." SB/SE Division management stated that the SB/SE Division Leadership Planning Committee developed the video and the SB/SE Division Commissioner approved the video.

No documentation was maintained to determine any costs associated with the "SB/SE Shuffle" video. Based on the estimated production costs previously discussed, we estimate that approximately $1,591 in staff time was necessary to produce this video. Our estimated costs for these videos exclude the time expended by SB/SE Division executives and managers when filming these videos.

Recommendation

Recommendation 6: The Chief Financial Officer should establish procedures to clearly outline the need for and value provided by any conference videos for future conferences. The purpose and use of videos should be clearly detailed in any request for a conference and include the applicable costs in the approval request.

> **Management's Response:** The IRS agreed with this recommendation. In February 2013, the IRS created a Service-Wide Video Editorial Board to review and approve all video projects planned throughout the IRS with consideration to cost, topic, and tone. The reviews will include training and education videos, webinars, vignettes, *etc.*, for external placement (YouTube, IRS.gov, and related websites) and any other ad hoc taping projects, such as videos for use at IRS meetings and conferences. Part of the Service-Wide Video Editorial Board's efforts will be focused on ensuring that internal and external videos have a sound business purpose and advance tax administration interests, either through taxpayer education or internal training.

A Substantial Number of Internal Revenue Service Employees Received Hotel Upgrades

As part of the Letters of Intent with the hotels, the IRS received a certain number of free rooms per night as well as suite upgrades that were used by IRS personnel. Federal employees traveling for work are paid for their lodging costs plus a fixed amount for meals (per diem). As part of the agreement, the hotels charged the IRS the Federal Government rate of $135 per night for all rooms (including suites) provided.

Specifically, the Letters of Intent indicate that 93 suite upgrades were provided by the Hilton, 33 by the Marriott, and six by the Sheraton each night of the conference. This represents 4.7 percent of the 2,830 rooms that the hotels agreed to reserve in the Letters of Intent.

Although the per diem rate of $135 was charged by the hotels, we determined the rack rates[13] for the upgraded rooms provided ranged from $299 per night to $1,500 per night, depending on the room and the hotel. For example, the Commissioner, SB/SE Division, stayed five nights in a Presidential Suite at the Marriott. This room is described as having a private bedroom, living area, conference table, wet bar, and billiard table. We spoke with a Marriott representative who stated that this suite currently retails for $3,500 per night.[14]

The Deputy Commissioner, SB/SE Division, stayed five nights in a two-bedroom Presidential Suite at the Hilton. The IRS paid the standard per diem rate of $135 per night for the room, which would have normally cost guests $1,499 per night during a four night stay. Figure 3 shows a Presidential Suite at the Hilton hotel.

Figure 3: A Presidential Suite at the Hilton Hotel

Photo Removed Due to Copyright Restrictions

Source: Hilton website shown with permission from the Hilton Hotels and Resorts.

---

[13] "Rack rate" is a hotel industry term for the price a hotel charges for a room before any discount has been taken into account.
[14] The Marriott Hotel and Resorts declined our request to show an image of a Presidential Suite at the Anaheim Marriott from their website.

Per the Letters of Intent, the IRS negotiated to receive 10 complimentary rooms per night available among the three participating hotels. These rooms were used primarily by the paid speakers and non-IRS technical support staff. In addition, the two event planners were provided complimentary rooms for a total of 19 nights, and two local employees were each provided complimentary rooms for six nights.

Because these free rooms and upgrades were part of the Letters of Intent with the hotels, they are not gifts to employees. However, the solicitation and use of hotel room upgrades increases the perception of wasteful spending and should be carefully considered in the future.

Recommendation

Recommendation 7: The Chief Financial Officer should evaluate whether the solicitation of hotel room suite upgrades for use by IRS employees should be allowed in agreements with hotels hosting IRS conferences in the future. In addition, any agreement with hotels containing hotel suite upgrades should be approved by the applicable business unit executive.

> **Management's Response:** The IRS agreed with this recommendation. The Human Capital Office will update Internal Revenue Manual 6.410.1, *Leadership and Education, Selection of Off-Site Locations and Facilities for Training,* to prohibit the solicitation of room suite upgrades and to require approval by the applicable business unit executive when upgrades are offered at no cost to the IRS. The Agency-Wide Shared Services Procurement office will update and reissue Policy and Procedures Memorandum No. 70.24, *Acquiring Training, Meeting and Conference Space,* to prohibit the solicitation of room suite upgrades and to require approval by the applicable business unit executive when upgrades are offered at no cost to the IRS.

Local Employees Were Granted Authorization to Stay at the Conference Hotels

IRS travel guidelines allow employees on official travel more than 40 miles from both their official duty station and residence to claim per diem expenses.[15] These guidelines outline several circumstances that may justify an exception, such as when an employee is attending training or a conference and the location is at least 30 miles from both their official duty station and residence. Travel guidelines state that any per diem expenses (including lodging) are taxable to the employee if they are incurred within the local commuting area.

After the Anaheim conference was approved in April 2010, the SB/SE Division Commissioner authorized local employees the option of staying overnight at the conference hotels, regardless of

---

[15] The per diem allowance (also referred to as subsistence allowance) is a daily payment instead of reimbursement for actual expenses for lodging, meals, and related incidental expenses.

their post of duty. This decision was made to reduce the demands on local travelers who would otherwise experience lengthy commutes daily during the conference and to foster employee morale and team spirit.

The IRS provided us with a list of 38 local IRS employees who stayed at the hotels and incurred per diem expenses of $29,364. Additionally, we identified seven other local area employees who stayed at the Anaheim hotels and incurred per diem expenses totaling $4,816 who the IRS did not report on the list provided.

Because per diem expenses are taxable to the employees in the local commuting area, we asked the IRS to identify the employees who received a Form W-2, *Wage and Tax Statement*, reporting the taxable per diem. IRS management informed us that four of the 38 employees they knew had performed local travel were not issued a Form W-2 as required. In addition, IRS management agreed that two of the seven additional employees we identified incurred taxable travel expenses and were not issued Forms W-2. They disagreed with the other five because they believe the employees' residences and posts of duty were more than 30 miles from the conference location. However, our research indicated that the posts of duty for these employees were within 30 miles of the conference location. As a result, we believe that these employees incurred taxable travel.

Recommendation

Recommendation 8: The Chief Financial Officer should identify all local employees who claimed per diem travel related to the conference and ensure that Forms W-2 are issued to all employees for taxable travel as appropriate.

> **Management's Response:** The IRS agreed with this recommendation. The IRS will identify local employees who did not receive a Form W-2 for taxable travel and will issue them as appropriate.

Several Meals and a Welcome Reception Were Provided During the Conference

As part of its agreement with the Anaheim hotels, the IRS required certain concessions including several food and beverage requests. This included the following items that were contracted to be served during the conference: a welcome reception with cocktails (each attendee was provided two free drink coupons), salad, appetizers, fajitas, pasta, and dessert; a daily continental breakfast consisting of two bread items, whole fruits, juice, tea, and coffee; and beverages and snacks during morning and afternoon breaks.

In addition to their lodging costs, Federal employees traveling for work are paid a fixed amount for meals (per diem). In Calendar Year 2010, the meal and incidental expenses allowance for Anaheim, California, was $71 per day. According to the Federal Travel Regulations, employees are not required to reduce their per diem reimbursement for complimentary meals provided by a hotel or motel.

Other Expenses Related to the Conference

During our review, we identified other questionable expenses related to the conference. These expenses related to the use of an "information corridor" staffed by IRS employees from various IRS business units during the conference, gifts and/or promotional items provided to conference attendees, and a contract for automated response tools used by attendees during the conference.

An exhibitor hall was used at significant additional cost

An information corridor, *i.e.*, exhibitor hall, was established at the conference where "representatives from various offices within the IRS could share information on their services and share hands-on demos with meeting participants." IRS documentation indicated that there were 41 booths at the information corridor staffed by IRS employees from various business units as well as non-IRS employees. Specifically:

- 42 IRS employees traveled for the information corridor (seven SB/SE Division employees and 35 non-SB/SE Division employees). The IRS reported more than $44,000 in total travel related to the information corridor.

- Examples of some booths at the information corridor included: the IRS Employee Recognition Program; Equal Employment Opportunity/Diversity personnel; the IRS Recruitment Office; the Wellness Program; the Federal Managers Association; Worker's Compensation; and USAJobs/CareerConnector.

- Per the IRS website,

  The exhibit featured engaging activities, such as an outer space galaxy challenge giveaway, Los Angeles Angels baseball ticket giveaway, and a time capsule (to share visions of SB/SE in 2020), as well as booths, displays, and an assortment of information about the work of SB/SE. The Information Galaxy was attended by over 1,800 individuals who visited booths hosted by SB/SE operating units and other IRS business units, executives, and senior managers. In addition to the Information Galaxy, it featured networking opportunities, educational workshops and forward-looking technology.

- At the information corridor, 24 tickets to two Los Angeles Angels baseball games (12 tickets per game) were used as contest prizes. SB/SE Division management advised us that these tickets were donated by the Hilton, the Marriott, and the Anaheim Convention and Visitors Bureau. They also stated that it is common industry practice for items to be donated to groups that hold large events in a particular city. IRS management stated that they relied upon advice from IRS Chief Counsel personnel for the appropriate treatment of these tickets.

The use of an information corridor and the associated costs were not clearly delineated in the request for the conference approved by the Deputy Commissioners.

Promotional items/gifts were provided to IRS employees

Numerous gifts/trinkets were provided to attendees at an estimated cost of more than $64,000. During our review, we noted that IRS employees attending the conference were provided with the following items per IRS documentation:

- 2,804 "brief bags" with an imprinted logo were provided to all attendees at an estimated cost of $15,669. The logo on each bag included the caption "Leading into the Future," the theme of the conference.

- 2,800 hard-covered spiral journals with a conference logo imprinted on the front and the hotels' and event planners' logos on the inside cover. The IRS paid $2,449 for 505 journals, with an additional $13,064 paid by the hotels, the event planners, and the Anaheim Convention and Visitors Bureau.

- 800 lanyards, 75 travel mugs, and 75 picture frames/clocks with the SB/SE Division logo, along with an unknown number of imprinted portfolios, sticky note pads, bookmarks, and retractable badge holders with a reported cost totaling approximately $19,210.

- Various promotional items totaling approximately $27,000 were provided at the information corridor booths. These included items such as "engraved pens/badge holders, give-away items from Oriental Trading,[16] promotional pens/printing poster/web cams, and imprinted can coolers/post-it notes."

We did not identify any guidance at the time of the conference outlining the purchase of gift items/mementos for conferences sponsored by the IRS. In August 2011, the IRS issued guidance to its senior executive staff discontinuing the purchase of any promotional items with logos or customized slogans, such as pens, mouse pads, mugs, and lanyards. The Deputy Commissioner for Operations Support or the Deputy Commissioner for Services and Enforcement must approve any exceptions to this policy. In October 2012, the IRS incorporated this guidance into its internal procedures manual.

Automated response tools were rented

The IRS also rented approximately 2,800 automated (audience) response tools at a cost of $24,828. SB/SE Division management advised us that their purpose was to provide an interactive training tool that would allow the speaker to gather results in real-time and share with

---

[16] These items were purchased by the Human Capital Office for approximately $730 and were given to attendees at the information corridor as well as during a conference workshop. They consisted of various items, including key chains, plastic coins, miniature stuffed animals, plastic squirting fish, and miniature bendable plastic figures.

participants. While the automated response tools may have provided some benefit to gauge audience participation, it was not used for CPE.

We reviewed the sessions that were recorded on 32 Digital Video Discs by the hotels during the conference and determined that the automated response tools were used for a total of 127 questions. However, a number of the questions were trivial in nature and were not intended to enhance attendees' knowledge of SB/SE Division operations. For example, the tools were used for 53 questions on the first day of the conference, mainly for an interactive "Jeopardy"-style game to quiz attendees on items covered in prior sessions or available in the information corridor. It appears the automated response tools were not used during the second day of the conference. On the last day, it was used for 74 questions during two sessions.

Recommendation

Recommendation 9: The Chief Financial Officer should establish procedures to clearly outline the need for and value provided by any information corridors/exhibitor halls and other technology for future conferences. The purpose and use of any exhibitor hall or technology should be clearly detailed in any request for a conference and include the applicable costs, including giveaway items, in the approval request.

> **Management's Response:** The IRS agreed with this recommendation. The Chief Financial Officer issued the December 27, 2012, Interim Guidance Memorandum, *Reissued Interim Guidance on the Approval Process for Event-Related Spending,* which outlines the requirements to include the full cost of events when submitting events for approval. The Human Capital Office will update IRM 6.410.1, *Leadership and Education, Selection of Off-Site Locations and Facilities for Training,* to reflect guidance on the analysis of the use of exhibitor halls and specialized technology.

Appendix I

Detailed Objective, Scope, and Methodology

The overall objective of this review was to identify the IRS's spending on conferences during FYs 2010 through 2012. One conference was selected to determine whether it was properly approved and the expenditures were appropriate. Although our primary focus was the August 2010 SB/SE Division's All Managers Conference in Anaheim, California, we also surveyed other IRS conferences held during FYs 2010 through 2012. To accomplish our objective, we:

I.   Reviewed the applicable Federal and IRS guidelines for spending on conferences.

II.   Obtained a complete list of conferences[1] held by the IRS for FYs 2010 through 2012.

   A. Identified conferences hosted by the IRS that may warrant review based upon specific allegations provided to the Treasury Inspector General for Tax Administration, estimated cost, location, number of attendees, cost per conference and attendee, *etc.*

   B. Requested additional information from the IRS for selected conferences. (We reviewed detailed cost information related only to the Anaheim conference.)

III.   For the Anaheim conference, reviewed the process used by the IRS to determine whether the required information and support was included in the request for approval.

IV.   Evaluated the costs incurred for the Anaheim conference to determine whether the expenditures were appropriate and reasonable.

   A. Obtained documentation to calculate the costs charged on IRS travel vouchers by attendees at the conference.

   B. Obtained and reviewed documentation from the IRS detailing expenditures to determine whether they were excessive or inappropriate.

   C. Determined whether IRS employees attending the conference received complimentary meals and lodging tax exemptions from the conference hotels.

   D. Determined whether local employees who stayed in the conference hotels received a taxable benefit and were authorized to charge the Government for lodging.

---

[1] For this audit, we defined conferences as an IRS-sponsored meeting, retreat, seminar, symposium, or event that involved travel for 50 or more attendees.

E. Estimated the total amount received by outside speakers and event planners based on their services.

F. Reviewed available documentation to determine whether planning trips were made for the conference and the total costs associated with these trips.

G. Determined whether any IRS employees received awards based on work supporting the conference and, if so, the amount and justification.

H. Discussed potential exceptions, such as questionable/excessive costs, with applicable IRS management.

Internal controls methodology

Internal controls relate to management's plans, methods, and procedures used to meet their mission, goals, and objectives. Internal controls include the processes and procedures for planning, organizing, directing, and controlling program operations. They include the systems for measuring, reporting, and monitoring program performance. We determined the following internal controls were relevant to our audit objective: the IRS's approval process for conferences and the IRS's policy for off-site events. We evaluated these controls by interviewing IRS management, reviewing a sample of travel vouchers, and reviewing other applicable documentation for the Anaheim conference.

Appendix II

Major Contributors to This Report

Gregory D. Kutz, Assistant Inspector General for Audit (Management Services and Exempt Organizations)
Jeffrey M. Jones, Director
Jonathan T. Meyer, Director
Alicia P. Mrozowski, Director
Heather M. Hill, Audit Manager
Janice M. Pryor, Audit Manager
Mary F. Herberger, Lead Auditor
LaToya R. Penn, Senior Auditor
Gary D. Pressley, Senior Auditor
Joseph P. Smith, Senior Auditor

Appendix III

Report Distribution List

Acting Commissioner C
Office of the Commissioner – Attn: Chief of Staff C
Deputy Commissioner for Operations Support OS
Deputy Commissioner for Services and Enforcement SE
Commissioner, Small Business/Self-Employed Division SE:S
Deputy Chief Financial Officer OS:CFO
Director, Strategy and Finance, Small Business/Self-Employed Division SE:S:SF
Chief Counsel CC
National Taxpayer Advocate TA
Director, Office of Program Evaluation and Risk Analysis RAS:O
Office of Internal Control OS:CFO:CPIC:IC
Director, Office of Legislative Affairs CL:LA
Audit Liaisons:
    Commissioner, Small Business/Self-Employed Division SE:S
    Chief Financial Officer OS:CFO

Appendix IV

Internal Revenue Service Conferences Held During Fiscal Years 2010 Through 2012[1]

FY	Name	Division	Estimated Cost	Attendees	Venue	Location
2010	SB/SE All Managers CPE	SB/SE	$4,133,183	2,609	Marriott/Hilton/ Sheraton	Anaheim, CA
2010	SB/SE Exam CPE FY 2010	SB/SE	$3,180,412	3,892	Various IRS locations & private space	Approx. 60 various cities
2010	TAS Technical Training Symposium	TAS	$2,933,042	2,113	Philadelphia Marriott	Philadelphia, PA
2010	SB/SE Collection Leadership CPE	SB/SE	$1,198,397	721	Manchester Grand Hyatt	San Diego, CA
2010	LB&I (LMSB) All Managers Meeting	LB&I	$1,181,871	800	Marriott Marquis Hotel	Atlanta, GA
2010	SB/SE Technical Training	Counsel	$1,158,628	665	Chicago Hyatt Regency	Chicago, IL
2010	SB/SE Collection Administrative Professional CPE	SB/SE	$909,792	813	Atlanta Marriott Marquis	Atlanta, GA
2010	SB CPE: Bank Secrecy Act Program CPE	SB/SE	$786,939	527	Downtown Marriott	Chicago, IL
2010	FY 2010 CPE for Exam Secretaries	SB/SE	$746,994	562	Kansas City Marriott Hotel	Kansas City, MO
2010	LMSB Technical Training	Counsel	$638,635	433	Chicago Hyatt Regency	Chicago, IL
2010	Appeals Processing Services CPE	Appeals	$637,930	382	Westin Michigan Avenue	Chicago, IL
2010	Excise Revenue Agent CPE 2010	SB/SE	$610,717	450	Marriott	Anaheim, CA
2010	Employment Tax Specialists CPE 2010	SB/SE	$589,142	410	Omni San Diego Hotel	San Diego, CA

---

[1] Abbreviations used in this table are defined in Appendix V.

FY	Name	Division	Estimated Cost	Attendees	Venue	Location
2010	GE CPE	TE/GE	$529,863	368	Sheraton Hotel	Denver, CO
2010	AWSS All Managers CPE	AWSS	$498,000	277	Marriott Hotel	New Orleans, LA
2010	Settlement Officers CPE Field	Appeals	$463,076	308	Westin Canal Place	New Orleans, LA
2010	All Managers Meeting	Appeals	$400,411	246	Intercontinental Hotel	Chicago, IL
2010	LMSB Support Staff CPE	LB&I	$381,113	300	Crown Plaza Riverwalk	San Antonio, TX
2010	Abusive Transactions Summit Training	SB/SE	$358,938	238	Manchester Grand Hyatt	San Diego, CA
2010	CI Supervisory Special Agent Workshops	CI	$351,413	224	Westin City Center	Dallas, TX
2010	EP Rulings and Agreements Annual CPE	TE/GE	$318,656	306	Hyatt Regency	Indianapolis, IN
2010	Business Master File Revenue Officer Training	Appeals	$316,031	134	Hilton	Memphis, TN
2010	IT Services Leadership Conference	MITS	$307,187	320	Millennium Hotel	Cincinnati, OH
2010	New Hire Orientation – Settlement Officers Session 2	Appeals	$301,771	230	Crowne Plaza Dallas	Dallas, TX
2010	New Attorney Orientation	Counsel	$263,577	190	Grand Hyatt	Washington, D.C.
2010	Taxpayer Advocacy Panel Annual Meeting	TAS	$263,275	136	Capital Hilton	Washington, D.C.
2010	EO Basic New Hire Training	TE/GE	$260,765	89	Harris Tower	Atlanta, GA
2010	TAS Leadership Conference	TAS	$259,212	127	Washington Marriott Metro Center	Washington, D.C.
2010	Specialty Managers CPE	SB/SE	$248,463	126	Sheraton Riverwalk Hotel	Tampa, FL
2010	Congressional Affairs Program Conference	TAS	$243,705	123	Capital Hilton	Washington, D.C.
2010	IRS Nationwide Tax Forums	C&L	$242,331	259	Mandalay Bay	Las Vegas, NV
2010	Technical Services Tax Examiner CPE	SB/SE	$225,874	211	Crowne Plaza Riverwalk	San Antonio, TX
2010	IRS Nationwide Tax Forums	C&L	$223,618	239	Hilton	Atlanta, GA

FY	Name	Division	Estimated Cost	Attendees	Venue	Location
2010	IRS Nationwide Tax Forums	C&L	$222,682	238	Hilton	New York, NY
2010	GLS Technical Training	Counsel	$218,877	84	Chicago Hyatt Regency	Chicago, IL
2010	All Managers Meeting – EUES	MITS	$212,540	126	Hilton	Atlanta, GA
2010	IRS Nationwide Tax Forums	C&L	$208,648	223	Town & Country Hotel & Conf. Center	San Diego, CA
2010	IRS Nationwide Tax Forums	C&L	$206,776	221	Hyatt	Chicago, IL
2010	SCR/Administrative Officer CPE	AWSS	$205,000	120	Hilton	San Francisco, CA
2010	CPE	AWSS	$201,215	142	Omni La Mansion	San Antonio, TX
2010	CPE	AWSS	$200,110	138	Omni La Mansion	San Antonio, TX
2010	IRS Nationwide Tax Forums	C&L	$189,935	203	Caribe Royale	Orlando, FL
2010	Research CPE	SB/SE	$187,651	107	Omni Hotel	San Diego, CA
2010	S&F Face to Face CPE	SB/SE	$184,853	126	Sheraton Gunter Hotel	San Antonio, TX
2010	Specialty Administrative Professionals CPE	SB/SE	$184,835	81	Crown Plaza	San Antonio, TX
2010	Accounts Management Analyst Technical Training	W&I	$182,311	139	Renaissance Hotel Downtown	Atlanta, GA
2010	BMO All Employees CPE	W&I	$178,146	180	Sheraton	Atlanta, GA
2010	EOps All Managers Meeting	MITS	$171,573	185	Martinsburg Computing Ctr.	Martinsburg, WV
2010	All Employees CPE	AWSS	$166,431	150	Intercontinental Hotel	Dallas, TX
2010	FY 2010 CPE for Fraud Technical Advisors	SB/SE	$163,009	101	Blackstone Renaissance	Chicago, IL
2010	All Managers CPE	AWSS	$160,121	77	Wyndam Virginia Crossing Hotel	Richmond, VA
2010	TE/GE Technical Training	Counsel	$158,372	132	Hyatt Regency	Chicago, IL
2010	ERCS Oracle Discover	SB/SE	$154,076	74	Kansas City Campus	Kansas City, MO
2010	FM Manager Training	Counsel	$152,781	90	Chicago Hyatt Regency	Chicago, IL

FY	Name	Division	Estimated Cost	Attendees	Venue	Location
2010	CI Narcotics Money Laundering Training Seminar	CI	$145,306	106	El Paso Intelligence Center	El Paso, TX
2010	CI Chicago Field Office CPE Conference	CI	$140,937	180	Weston Hotel	Indianapolis, IN
2010	2010 IRS Research Conference	RAS	$140,893	350	The Liaison Capitol Hill	Washington, D.C.
2010	CT Technical Training	Counsel	$140,496	87	Chicago Hyatt Regency	Chicago, IL
2010	Systems Integration and Coordination Branch All Hands Meeting – EOps	MITS	$134,834	91	Tennessee Computing Ctr.	Memphis, TN
2010	California All Managers Meeting	SB/SE	$134,608	130	Hilton	San Jose, CA
2010	CI Warrants and Forfeiture Asset Forfeiture CPE	CI	$131,291	130	Fort Lauderdale	Ft. Lauderdale, FL
2010	Strategy and Finance Analyst CPE	Appeals	$127,501	106	Hilton Memphis	Memphis, TN
2010	SB/SE Area Hiring Coordinator Planning Meeting	SB/SE	$127,500	86	Chicago Hilton Suites	Chicago, IL
2010	Field Specialist Issue Focus Meeting	LB&I	$126,685	86	San Diego Marriott	San Diego, CA
2010	CI Seattle Field Office CPE	CI	$125,579	127	Hilton Garden Inn	Seattle, WA
2010	W&I Compliance Headquarters Analysts Conference	W&I	$121,689	140	Ritz Carlton	Atlanta, GA
2010	Settlement Officers CPE Campus (East)	Appeals	$120,763	130	Hilton	Memphis, TN
2010	Exam Midwest Area All Managers Meeting	SB/SE	$120,415	96	Embassy Suites Hotel	Indianapolis, IN
2010	New Hire Orientation (AOs) – Session I	Appeals	$119,004	116	Crown Plaza	Dallas, TX
2010	EP Examinations 403(b) Training	TE/GE	$118,874	90	Embassy Suites	Phoenix, AZ
2010	M&F All Employees Meeting	LB&I	$117,546	87	The Admiral Fell Inn	Baltimore, MD
2010	BSA Conference	CI	$114,000	76	Benson Hotel	Portland, OR

FY	Name	Division	Estimated Cost	Attendees	Venue	Location
2010	SPEC National Disability Institute (NDI) Mayor Conference	W&I	$113,857	111	City Library	Jacksonville, FL
2010	Appeals Officers Campus CPE	Appeals	$113,476	110	Crowne Plaza West	Philadelphia, PA
2010	Annual Business Meeting	NHQ	$112,753	340	Westin Arlington Gateway	Arlington, VA
2010	Basic Trial Advocacy	Counsel	$112,729	53	Dallas CDS Training Site	Dallas, TX
2010	Exam Gulf States Area All Managers Meeting	SB/SE	$111,854	147	DoubleTree	Dallas, TX
2010	EO Exam All Managers Meeting	TE/GE	$111,733	73	Embassy Suites	Chicago, IL
2010	IRS Training Class – Phase II	CI	$110,586	77	Sea Palms Hotel	St. Simons, GA
2010	Basic Trial Advocacy	Counsel	$109,557	53	Dallas CDS Training Site	Dallas, TX
2010	Financial Management Customer Training Conference	CFO	$109,165	98	Tamarack Conference Center	Beckley, WV
2010	Exam South Atlantic All Managers Meeting	SB/SE	$106,896	121	Marriott	Lake Mary, FL
2010	Appeals Regional Meeting	Appeals	$105,567	85	Wyndham Hotel	Chicago, IL
2010	EPTA CPE	TE/GE	$104,573	68	Hotel Monaco	Seattle, WA
2010	IRS-CI/TEOAF Title 31/SAR Review Task Force	CI	$102,501	137	Omni Shoreham	San Diego, CA
2010	Atlanta Accounts Management Leadership Conference	W&I	$101,342	172	Wyndam Riverwalk Hotel	Jacksonville, FL
2010	Corporate New Hire Orientation Sep 10 TCO	SB/SE	$100,114	87	Hilton/Westin	Anaheim, CA, and Atlanta, GA
2010	North Atlantic Area All Managers CPE	CI	$100,000	82	Wyndham Princeton Forrestal Hotel	Princeton, NJ
2010	SPEC Leadership Conference	W&I	$99,947	70	Twelve Centennial	Atlanta, GA

FY	Name	Division	Estimated Cost	Attendees	Venue	Location
2010	Basic Trial Advocacy	Counsel	$99,092	53	New Carrollton Federal Bldg.	Lanham, MD
2010	Exam North Atlantic Area All Managers Meeting	SB/SE	$98,877	112	Westin Hotel	Providence, RI
2010	CI National Counterterrorism Seminar	CI	$98,000	85	Shades of Green	Orlando, FL
2010	LMSB Managers Meeting	Counsel	$97,000	77	Embassy Suites	Tampa, FL
2010	Exam Western Area All Managers Meeting	SB/SE	$96,497	92	Heathman Lodge	Vancouver, WA
2010	Personnel Security CPE	HCO	$95,831	75	Pittsburgh Marriot City Center	Pittsburgh, PA
2010	M&P Leadership Conference	W&I	$95,820	62	Bolger Center	Potomac, MD
2010	BSP Conference	AWSS	$95,693	84	DoubleTree	Orlando, FL
2010	Commissioner Leadership Conference	W&I	$94,249	120	Georgia Tech Hotel	Atlanta, GA
2010	Cross-Functional International Training	TE/GE	$94,179	58	Park Hyatt	Washington, D.C.
2010	Training – EOps	MITS	$93,665	73	New Carrollton Federal Bldg.	Lanham, MD
2010	PIPDS All Employees Meeting	PGLD	$90,804	65	Hyatt Regency	Savannah, GA
2010	SB/SE Collection Gulf States All Managers Meeting	SB/SE	$90,000	95	Crowne Plaza Hotel	Dallas, TX
2010	Corporate New Hire Orientation – April 10 TCO	SB/SE	$89,772	76	Westin Hotel	Dallas, TX
2010	All Managers CPE	HCO	$89,540	50	Marriott Copley Plaza	Boston, MA
2010	Exam Technical Service All Managers Meeting	SB/SE	$88,837	55	Hyatt Regency	Chicago, IL
2010	All Managers Meeting	HCO	$88,824	50	Westin Memphis Beale Hotel	Memphis, TN
2010	Appeals TG Business Meeting	Appeals	$88,419	70	Hyatt Regency Baltimore	Baltimore, MD
2010	PIO CPE	CI	$87,483	67	Hotel Solamar	San Diego, CA
2010	Exam Central Area All Managers Meeting	SB/SE	$87,089	70	DoubleTree Hotel and Suites	Pittsburgh, PA

FY	Name	Division	Estimated Cost	Attendees	Venue	Location
2010	Newark Field Office FY10 CPE	CI	$87,084	107	Thayer Hotel	West Point, NJ
2010	Oakland Field Office FY10 CPE	CI	$85,752	132	DoubleTree Hotel	Rohnert Park, CA
2010	CPE for IMD Community	RAS	$85,274	193	Georgetown University	New Carrollton, MD
2010	Fraud Technical Advisors Revenue Agent International	SB/SE	$84,424	153	St. Louis Union Station Marriott	St. Louis, MO
2010	CLD Administrative CPE	SB/SE	$83,276	55	Hyatt	Baltimore, MD
2010	EP Examinations Programs and Review CPE	TE/GE	$81,842	60	Nashville CDS	Nashville, TN
2010	Technical Advisors CPE	Appeals	$81,350	61	IRS Appeals Office	Washington, D.C.
2010	CI Refund Crimes All Managers Meeting	CI	$79,675	67	Hilton Charlotte University Place	Charlotte, NC
2010	Advanced Trial Advocacy	Counsel	$77,679	55	Jacksonville CDS Training Site	Jacksonville, FL
2010	Area 10 Business Meeting	Appeals	$77,175	126	Holiday Inn – Airport	Fresno, CA
2010	Account Managers FY11 Leadership Conference	W&I	$77,072	201	Marriott South	Austin, TX
2010	FA Area 4 Leadership Conference	W&I	$74,588	53	Omni	Houston, TX
2010	EP MAP Training	TE/GE	$74,276	56	IRS Office	Jacksonville, FL
2010	FBSA Secretary CPE 2010	SB/SE	$73,981	54	St. Louis Union Station Marriott	St Louis, MO
2010	All Managers Meeting	CFO	$72,195	54	Airlie Center	Warrenton, VA
2010	Account Managers Fresno Directorate Leadership Conference	W&I	$71,959	87	Courtyard Marriott	Portland, OR
2010	Detroit Field Office FY10 CPE	CI	$67,338	95	Marriott	East Lansing, MI
2010	EP Conflict Management	TE/GE	$66,778	57	Chet Holifield Federal Building	Philadelphia, PA

FY	Name	Division	Estimated Cost	Attendees	Venue	Location
2010	CCS Filing and Payment Compliance	SB/SE	$66,000	55	Hyatt Regency	St. Louis, MO
2010	FA Area 3 Leadership Conference	W&I	$65,962	53	Hyatt	Atlanta, GA
2010	W&I Compliance Leadership Conference	W&I	$64,805	60	Georgia Tech Hotel	Atlanta, GA
2010	Reasonable Accommodations	AWSS	$63,961	50	DoubleTree	Dallas, TX
2010	National Research Project Training	TE/GE	$63,812	58	Nashville CDS	Nashville, TN
2010	FA Area 2 Leadership Conference	W&I	$63,548	56	Gateway Center	Cincinnati, OH
2010	EPSS Leadership Conference	W&I	$62,193	60	Renaissance	Atlanta, GA
2010	SB:SP:EG Estate and Gift Tax Managers CPE 2010	SB/SE	$61,227	55	Marriott Waterside Hotel and Marina	Tampa, FL
2010	Andover Compliance Service Leadership Conference	W&I	$59,082	75	Nashua Radisson Castle	Nashua, NH
2010	CPE for IMD Community	RAS	$56,984	144	New Carrolton Federal Building	Kansas City, KS
2010	Compliance FY10 Leadership Conference	W&I	$53,580	140	Grand Occasions	Fresno, CA
2010	FA Area 1 Leadership Conference	W&I	$52,421	52	Andover Campus	Andover, MA
2010	SB/SE Collection Central Area All Managers Meeting	SB/SE	$48,000	63	Fairfield Inn	Weirton, WV
2010	Accounts Management Leadership Conference	W&I	$47,849	86	The W Hotel	Atlanta, GA
2010	Accounts Management Leadership CPE	W&I	$46,230	170	Atlantis Marine World	Riverhead, NY
2010	All Employees CPE	HCO	$41,006	50	Wyndham Virginia Crossings	Glenn Allen, WV
2010	FY10 IRS Ogden Accounts Management Center All Managers CPE Speed of Trust	W&I	$36,197	121	Marriott	Ogden, UT
2010	SP Joint Leadership Conference	W&I	$27,568	64	Little America Hotel	Salt Lake City, UT

FY	Name	Division	Estimated Cost	Attendees	Venue	Location
2010	All Managers FY 10 Leadership Conference	W&I	$22,319	118	Marriott	Ogden, UT
2010	Accounts Management Leadership Conference	W&I	$22,160	90	Hilton Hotel	Memphis, TN
2010	Kansas City Compliance Leadership Conference	W&I	$20,496	200	John Knox Village	Lee's Summit, MO
2010	Compliance Leadership Conference	W&I	$17,730	139	Austin Marriot	Austin, TX
2010	Accounts Management CPE	W&I	$16,693	90	Memphis Campus	Memphis, TN
2010	Atlanta Field Compliance Services Leadership Conference	W&I	$16,274	139	Twelve Hotel	Atlanta, GA
2010	Accounts Management Training Day	W&I	$2,720	200	Tusculum Church of Christ	Nashville, TN
2011	Estate and Gift Tax Attorney FY 11 CPE	SB/SE	$480,638	332	Marriott Waterside Hotel and Marina	Tampa, FL
2011	IRS Nationwide Tax Forums	C&L	$261,721	277	Gaylord National Harbor	Washington, D.C.
2011	Taxpayer Advocacy Panel Annual Meeting	TAS	$260,600	136	Capital Hilton	Washington, D.C.
2011	TAS Leadership Conference	TAS	$258,005	113	Fairmont Hotel	Washington, D.C.
2011	Congressional Affairs Program Conference	TAS	$234,793	121	Fairmont Hotel	Washington, D.C.
2011	Fraud Technical Advisors Phase II (course delivery)	SB/SE	$211,312	78	Marriott Mission Valley	San Diego, CA
2011	IRS Nationwide Tax Forums	C&L	$205,975	218	Caesar's Palace	Las Vegas, NV
2011	Annual Asset Forfeiture CPE	CI	$204,925	130	W Scottsdale	Scottsdale, AZ
2011	Fraud Emerging International Issues	SB/SE	$186,730	155	St. Louis Union Station Marriott	St. Louis, MO
2011	All Managers Meeting – EUES	MITS	$180,969	111	Marriott Quorum	Dallas, TX
2011	All Managers Meeting	HCO	$179,044	145	Hyatt Regency Baltimore	Baltimore, MD
2011	IRS Nationwide Tax Forums	C&L	$178,575	189	Marriott	Atlanta, GA

FY	Name	Division	Estimated Cost	Attendees	Venue	Location
2011	IRS Nationwide Tax Forums	C&L	$167,237	177	Hilton	Dallas, TX
2011	New Hire Orientation (AOs)	Appeals	$161,731	144	DoubleTree Hotel	Dallas, TX
2011	IRS Nationwide Tax Forums	C&L	$159,678	169	San Jose Convention Center	San Jose, CA
2011	IRS Nationwide Tax Forums	C&L	$155,899	165	Hilton	Orlando, FL
2011	BSA Conference	CI	$153,000	102	Drake Hotel	Chicago, IL
2011	CI Senior Leadership Meeting	CI	$147,831	119	Sheraton Hotel	McLean, VA
2011	SB/SE Collection AIQ All Managers Meeting	SB/SE	$141,381	135	Hilton Indianapolis	Indianapolis, IN
2011	All Managers CPE	AWSS	$141,109	72	Wyndam Virginia Crossing Hotel	Richmond, VA
2011	Fuel Compliance Agent (FCA) Phase III	SB/SE	$134,106	59	Brentwood Training Center	Brentwood, TN
2011	All Managers Meeting	AWSS	$127,168	96	Baltimore Marriott	Baltimore, MD
2011	Senior Managers Meeting	HCO	$117,283	70	Park Plaza Hotel and Tower	Boston, MA
2011	CI Questionable Refund Program and RPP Meeting	CI	$109,759	84	Gallery One	Ft. Lauderdale, FL
2011	All Employees CPE	C&L	$100,835	72	Intercontinental	Chicago, IL
2011	NATIA Conference	CI	$99,099	54	Tampa Convention Ctr.	Tampa, FL
2011	Basic Trial Advocacy	Counsel	$97,561	53	Dallas CDS Training Site	Dallas, TX
2011	New Hire Orientation (Settlement Officers)	Appeals	$97,279	122	DoubleTree Hotel	Dallas, TX
2011	CI National Counterterrorism Seminar	CI	$91,311	77	Shades of Green	Orlando, FL
2011	Basic Trial Advocacy	Counsel	$90,057	53	Dallas CDS Training Site	Dallas, TX
2011	Leadership Conference	AWSS	$90,036	63	New York New York Hotel	Las Vegas, NV
2011	SPEC National Disability Institute Mayor Conference	W&I	$86,724	72	Federal Reserve	Boston, MA

FY	Name	Division	Estimated Cost	Attendees	Venue	Location
2011	CIMIS Equipment Coordinator CPE	CI	$83,000	58	Westin Canal Place Hotel	New Orleans, LA
2011	Domestic Terrorism and Frivolous Filer Training Conference	CI	$79,447	75	Sheraton Hotel	Chicago, IL
2011	New Attorney Orientation	Counsel	$77,063	85	IRS Main Building	Washington, D.C.
2011	EO International Training	TE/GE	$76,872	62	Nashville CDS	Nashville, TN
2011	Coordinated Issues Cases Excise Cases	SB/SE	$76,137	54	Brentwood Training Center	Brentwood, TN
2011	Asset Forfeiture Basic Training	CI	$76,117	66	Chet Holified Federal Building	Laguna Niguel, CA
2011	Issue Practice Group (CAM and DCE)	LB&I	$71,457	65	DoubleTree by Hilton, Buckhead	Atlanta, GA
2011	SB/SE Collection Midwest Area All Managers Meeting	SB/SE	$71,435	80	DoubleTree Milwaukee City Center	Milwaukee, WI
2011	PIPDS All Employees Meeting	PGLD	$68,611	72	Intercontinental Harbor Court	Baltimore, MD
2011	SPEC National Disability Institute (NDI) Mayor Conference	W&I	$62,206	111	Federal Reserve	Chicago, IL
2011	EP Voluntary Compliance Workshop	TE/GE	$60,712	87	DoubleTree Hotel	Austin, TX
2011	CI Asset Forfeiture Training Conference	CI	$27,180	78	Marriott Hotel	Kansas City, MO
2011	Charlotte Field Office Asset Forfeiture Training/Town Hall Meeting	CI	$22,804	85	Embassy Suites	Charlotte, NC
2011	Accounts Management FY11 Leadership Conference Continuous Improvement Starts With One	W&I	$21,515	126	Marriott	Ogden, UT
2011	Asset Forfeiture Conference – New Orleans Field Office	CI	$19,443	61	Oxford Conference Center	Oxford, MS
2011	Cincinnati SP Leadership Conference	W&I	$570	125	Gateway Center	Covington, KY

FY	Name	Division	Estimated Cost	Attendees	Venue	Location
2011	M&P Leadership Conference	W&I	$372	65	Video Conference	Video Conference
2012	Flow Through Entity	SB/SE	$1,778,194	317	IRS Space	Various Cities
2012	Flow Through Entity	SB/SE	$1,044,259	211	IRS Space	Various Cities
2012	EP Examinations Phase III New Hire Training	TE/GE	$218,871	61	Earle Cabell Federal Building	Dallas, TX
2012	Congressional Affairs Program Conference	TAS	$200,903	107	Fairmont Hotel	Washington, D.C.
2012	TAS Leadership Conference	TAS	$196,000	115	Hyatt Arlington	Arlington, VA
2012	New Hire Orientation for FY13	Appeals	$156,600	115	DoubleTree Hotel	Dallas, TX
2012	National Tax Forum	C&L	$146,358	81	Hilton	New York, NY
2012	National Tax Forum	C&L	$133,648	89	Caesar's Palace	Las Vegas, NV
2012	CI Refund Crimes CPE	CI	$133,415	96	Omni La Mansion Del Rio Hotel	San Antonio, TX
2012	National Tax Forum	C&L	$124,445	79	Hyatt McCormick Place	Chicago, IL
2012	National Tax Forum	C&L	$116,752	82	Hilton	Orlando, FL
2012	National Tax Forum	C&L	$106,220	78	Marriott	Atlanta, GA
2012	National Tax Forum	C&L	$102,933	78	Town and Country	San Diego, CA
2012	Advanced Training	CI	$99,586	70	King and Prince Hotel	St. Simons, GA
2012	PFTG QA Consistency Forum	LB&I	$75,000	50	IRS CDS Training Facility	Pittsburgh, PA
2012	LITC Grantee Conference	TAS	$72,563	60	Capitol Hilton	Washington, D.C.
2012	Fiduciary Abusive Trust	SB/SE	$61,684	50	Chet Holifield Federal Building	Laguna Niguel, CA
2012	New Attorney Orientation	Counsel	$53,362	103	IRS Main Building	Washington, D.C.
2012	Fresno SP Leadership Conference	W&I	$18,379	190	Golden Palace	Fresno, CA

FY	Name	Division	Estimated Cost	Attendees	Venue	Location
2012	Austin SP Leadership Conference	W&I	$8,366	180	Wyndham Hotel	Austin, TX
2012	Natural Resources and Construction Industry DFO – West Town Hall Meeting	LB&I	$5,000	175	Ronald Deaton Civic Auditorium	Los Angeles, CA
2012	Ogden SP Leadership Conference	W&I	$3,600	140	Davis Conference Center	Layton, UT
2012	Kansas City SP Leadership Conference	W&I	$669	160	Kansas City Campus	Kansas City, MO
2012	Compliance Leadership Conference	W&I	$0	110	Austin Campus	Austin, TX
Fiscal Year 2010 Estimated Cost	$37,567,680					
Fiscal Year 2011 Estimated Cost	$ 6,207,312					
Fiscal Year 2012 Estimated Cost	$ 4,856,807					
Grand Total Estimated Cost for 225 Conferences	**$48,631,799**					

Source: Chief Financial Officer, November 2012.[2]

[2] The Treasury Inspector General for Tax Administration has reviewed only the SB/SE Division Leadership Conference described in this report and has not performed any detailed analyses of the other conferences held during FYs 2010 through 2012.

Appendix V

Legend for Abbreviations Listed in Appendix IV

Acronym	Definition
AIQ	Advisory & Insolvency Quality
AO	Appeals Officer
AWSS	Agency-Wide Shared Services
BMO	Business Modernization Office
BSA	Bank Secrecy Act
BSP	Business System Planning
C&L	Communication & Liaison
CAM	Change in Accounting Method
CCS	Campus Compliance Services
CFO	Chief Financial Officer
CI	Criminal Investigation
CIMIS	Criminal Investigation Management Information System
CT	Criminal Tax
DCE	Detection Controlled Estimate
DFO	Director of Field Operations
EG	Estate and Gift Tax
EO	Exempt Organizations
EOps	Enterprise Operations
EP	Employee Plans
EPSS	Electronic Products & Services Support
EPTA	Employee Plans Team Audit
ERCS	Examination Return Control System
EUES	End User Equipment & Services
FA	Field Assistance
FM	Finance and Management
FO	Field Office
GE	Government Entity
GLS	General Legal Services

Acronym	Definition
HCO	Human Capital Office
IMD	Internal Management Documents
IT	Information Technology
LB&I	Large Business & International
LITC	Low Income Taxpayer Clinic
LMSB	Large and Midsize Business
M&F	Management and Finance
M&P	Media & Publications
MITS	Modernization & Information Technology Services
NATIA	National Technical Investigators' Association
NHQ	National Headquarters
PFTG	Prefiling Technical Guidance
PGLD	Privacy, Government Liaison, & Disclosure
PIO	Public Information Officer
PIPDS	Privacy, Information Protection, and Data Security
QA	Quality Assurance
RAS	Research Analysis Statistics
RPP	Return Preparer Program
S&F	Strategy and Finance
SAR	Suspicious Activity Report
SB	Small Business
SCR	Senior Commissioner Representative
SP	Submission Processing
SPEC	Stakeholder Partnership, Education, & Communication
TAS	Taxpayer Advocate Service
TCO	Tax Compliance Officer
TE/GE	Tax Exempt/Government Entities
TEOAF	Treasury Executive Officer of Asset Forfeiture
W&I	Wage & Investment

Source: IRS Intranet.

Appendix VI

Internal Revenue Service Conferences
Held During Fiscal Years 2010 Through 2012
Ranked by Highest Average Cost Per Event

IRS Operating Division	Number of Events	Total Cost	Average Cost Per Event
Taxpayer Advocate Service	10	$4,922,098	$492,210
SB/SE	44	$19,718,519	$448,148
Large Business and International	7	$1,958,672	$279,810
Chief Counsel	16	$3,545,466	$221,592
Appeals	16	$3,368,085	$210,505
Modernization and Information Technology Services	6	$1,100,768	$183,461
Agency-Wide Shared Services	11	$1,948,844	$177,168
Communication and Liaison	19	$3,254,266	$171,277
Tax Exempt and Government Entities	14	$2,181,806	$155,843
National Headquarters	1	$112,753	$112,753
Criminal Investigation	29	$3,173,861	$109,443
Human Capital Office	6	$611,528	$101,921
Research, Analysis, and Statistics	3	$283,151	$94,384
Chief Financial Officer	2	$181,360	$90,680
Office of Privacy, Government Liaison, and Disclosure	2	$159,415	$79,708
Wage and Investment	39	$2,111,208	$54,134
Totals	**225**	**$48,631,800**	**$216,141**

Source: Chief Financial Officer, November 2012.

Summary of Costs
for the Anaheim Conference

Category	Cost
Travel Including Lodging	$3,754,578
Guest Speakers	$135,350
Information Corridor Travel and Supplies	$71,381
Videos	$50,187
Miscellaneous/General Printing	$28,138
Automated Response Tools	$24,828
Brief Bags	$15,699
Folders	$12,763
Portfolios With Imprinted Logos	$10,209
Lanyards and Badge Holders	$6,060
Commissioner Awards Plaques	$4,500
Closed Captioning	$4,496
Books and Bookmarks	$3,076
Journals	$2,449
E-Ticket Card Decks	$2,072
Sign Language	$1,803
Engraved Travel Mugs and Clocks	$1,534
Miscellaneous Supplies	$1,169
Imprinted Sticky Note Pads	$1,165
Sleeves for Puzzle Pieces	$901
Digital Video Discs	$825
Total Costs	**$4,133,183**

Source: SB/SE Division management. Costs are rounded.

Appendix VIII

Guest Speakers Procured
for the Anaheim Conference

Guest Speaker	Cost	Service Provided	Topic
Frans Johannson	$27,500	Keynote Two Presentations	The Medici Effect
Erik Wahl	$17,000	Keynote Two Presentations	The Art of Vision
Shawn Anchor	$11,430	Four 90-Minute Workshops	Strategies for Increasing Employee Engagement
Steve Robbins	$10,822	Four 90-Minute Workshops	Unintentional Intolerance
John McCann	$8,983	Four 90-Minute Workshops	Courageous Decision Making & Rankism
Antony Bell	$8,917	Four 90-Minute Workshops	How Do I Become a Great Leader?
Dr. Timothy Clark	$8,802	Four 90-Minute Workshops	The Manager's Role in Implementing Change
Dr. Evan Offstein and Jay Morwick	$8,392	Four 90-Minute Workshops	Making Telework Work
Sharon Ellison	$7,000	Four 90-Minute Workshops	Talk Matters
Dr. Pete Hammett	$6,406	Four 90-Minute Workshops	Crisis Leadership
Dr. Jennifer Kahnweller	$5,512	Four 90-Minute Workshops	Leading With Quiet Confidence
John Wukovits	$4,864	Four 90-Minute Workshops	Eisenhower's Leadership
Mark Nishan	$3,500	Four 90-Minute Workshops	Positive Leadership
Dr. Mark Thurston	$3,222	Four 90-Minute Workshops	Mindfulness: A Pathway to Leadership
Vincent Stovall	$3,000	Four 90-Minute Workshops	Root Canal or Public Speaking?

Total Costs for Guest Speakers $135,350

Source: IRS sole-source justification documents; Standard Forms 182, Request, Authorization, Agreement & Certification of Training; and SB/SE Division management. Total costs are rounded up.

Appendix IX

Anaheim Conference Agenda

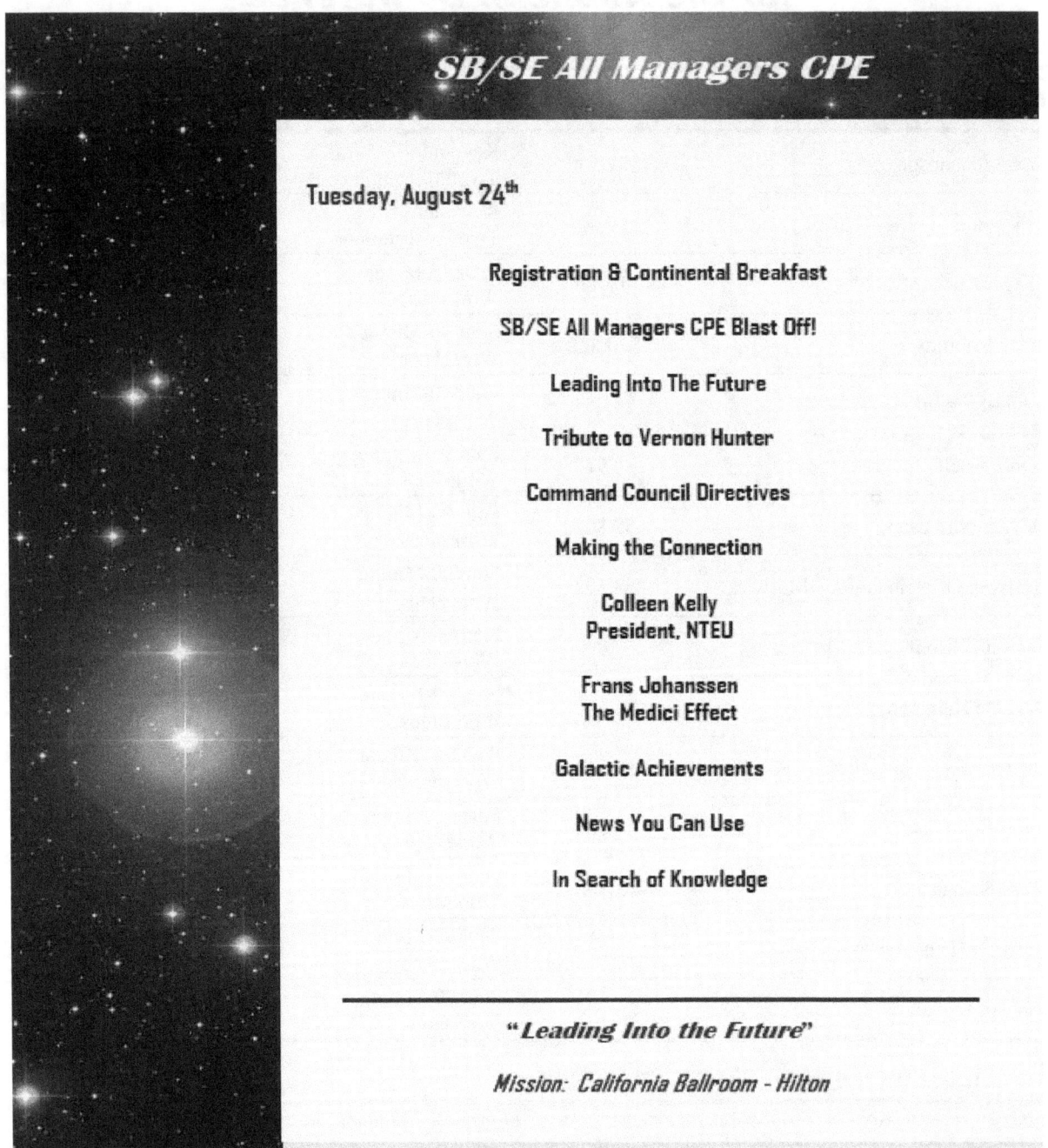

SB/SE All Managers CPE

Tuesday, August 24th

Registration & Continental Breakfast

SB/SE All Managers CPE Blast Off!

Leading Into The Future

Tribute to Vernon Hunter

Command Council Directives

Making the Connection

Colleen Kelly
President, NTEU

Frans Johanssen
The Medici Effect

Galactic Achievements

News You Can Use

In Search of Knowledge

"Leading Into the Future"

Mission: California Ballroom - Hilton

Anaheim Conference Agenda

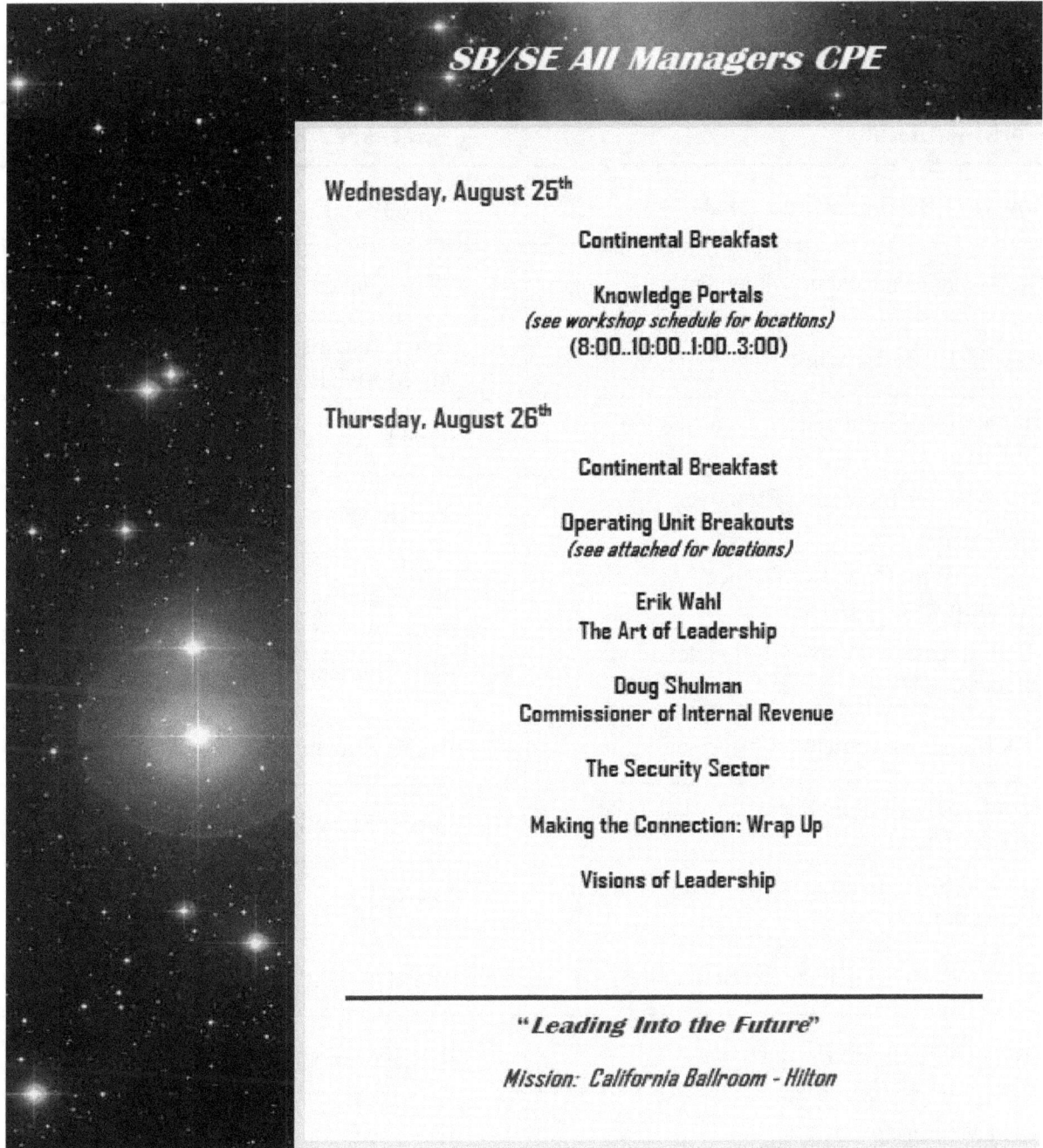

Source: SB/SE Division management.

Appendix X

Anaheim Conference Workshops
on August 25, 2010

Workshop Title	Speaker	Times
How Do I Become a Great Leader?	Antony Bell	8:00, 10:00, 1:00, 3:00
The Manager's Role in Implementing Change	Tim Clark	8:00, 10:00, 1:00, 3:00
Making Telework Work	Evan Offstein, Jay Morwich	8:00, 10:00, 1:00, 3:00
Unintentional Intolerance: Don't Be So N.I.C.E	Steve Robbins	8:00, 10:00, 1:00, 3:00
Strategies for Increasing Employee Engagement	Shawn Achor	8:00, 10:00, 1:00, 3:00
Leading With Quiet Confidence: The Introverted Leader	Jennifer Kahnweiler	8:00, 10:00, 1:00, 3:00
Mindfulness: A Pathway to Leadership Effectiveness	Mark Thurston	8:00, 10:00, 1:00, 3:00
Talk Matters! Authentic Conversations	Sharon Ellison	8:00, 10:00, 1:00, 3:00
Root Canal or Public Speaking – I'll Take the Root Canal	Vincent Stovall	8:00, 10:00, 1:00, 3:00
Political Savvy: How Not to Shoot Yourself in the Foot	IRS Speakers	8:00, 10:00, 1:00, 3:00
Why Doesn't Somebody Do Something?	Pete Hammett	8:00, 10:00, 1:00, 3:00
Creative Employee Engagement	IRS Speakers	8:00, 10:00, 1:00, 3:00
Flash Mentoring	IRS Speakers	8:00, 10:00, 1:00, 3:00

Workshop Title	Speaker	Times
Positive Leadership – Strategies for Extraordinary Performance	Mark Nishan	8:00, 10:00, 1:00, 3:00
Ike	John Wukovitz	8:00, 10:00, 1:00, 3:00
Connecting the Dots: Having a Customer Focus	IRS Speakers	1:00, 3:00
Writing Performance Reviews	IRS Speakers	8:00, 10:00, 1:00, 3:00
Is this Reasonable? Meeting the Needs of Your Employees	IRS Speakers	8:00, 10:00, 1:00, 3:00
Going Beyond, Beyond	IRS Speakers	8:00, 10:00, 1:00, 3:00
What's Hot, What's New, What's Going On	IRS Speakers	8:00, 10:00, 1:00, 3:00
Compliance Briefing: Updates on Current Tax Law and IRS Initiatives	IRS Speakers	8:00, 10:00, 1:00, 3:00
Strategic Thinking	IRS Speakers	8:00, 10:00, 1:00, 3:00
Rankism	John McCann	8:00, 10:00
Ethical Fitness	John McCann	1:00, 3:00

Source: SB/SE Division management.

Appendix XI

Management's Response to the Draft Report

April 29, 2013

MEMORANDUM FOR MICHAEL E. MCKENNEY
ACTING DEPUTY INSPECTOR GENERAL FOR AUDIT

FROM: Pamela J. LaRue
                Chief Financial Officer

SUBJECT: Draft Audit Report – Review of the August 2010 Small
                Business/Self-Employed Division's Conference in Anaheim,
                California (Audit # 201310024)

The IRS appreciates your review of the August 2010 Small Business/Self-Employed (SB/SE) Division's Manager Meeting. One year ago, when questions were raised with respect to the meeting, the IRS formally requested that the Treasury Inspector General for Tax Administration (TIGTA) review the meeting to determine that all IRS and government procedures were followed. We are pleased that TIGTA found no instances of fraud or violations of the Federal Acquisition Regulations.

The meeting took place at a time where the IRS needed to ensure that managers had proper training to address significant new programs, major staff and manager turnover and a substantial increase in security threats. However, since that time, the technology and budget environment has changed, and during the past three years, the IRS has put in place an extensive series of procedures with regard to conferences. Clearly, a conference like this from three years ago – and many of the instances described – would not take place under our expanded and strengthened oversight process. In addition, as discussed in more detail below, the IRS has elevated the conference approval processes so that all large meetings must be approved centrally and not solely by individual business units.

While more specifics regarding the meeting will be addressed below, it is important to note that in the three years since the meeting, the IRS has implemented comprehensive financial controls over meeting and conference approval processes and dramatically cut expenditures related to meetings and training. The expenditures related to this 2010 meeting are not reflective of the current spending environment at the IRS or the spending that has occurred over the last several years. As shown in the report, the number of large meetings decreased 84 percent between Fiscal Year (FY) 2010 and

2

FY 2012. The costs of these meetings decreased 87 percent over that time period. Costs for FY 2013 will be even lower.

Not only are costs for meetings and conferences significantly down since FY 2010, costs for all training-related travel were 68 percent lower from FY 2010 to FY 2012. To date, our travel and training expenses are down more than 80 percent since FY 2010. In fact, in FY 2012, more than 90 percent of our training courses were delivered virtually. Compared with FY 2010, the percentage of training hours delivered online has nearly doubled and our cost per hour of overall training has been reduced by 46 percent.

The IRS takes seriously our obligations to be good stewards of government resources. As detailed below, the IRS has instituted a number of procedures over the last three years that ensure sound financial decisions are being made in regard to spending. Since FY 2009, we have achieved $1 billion in budget savings and efficiencies.

With respect to the meeting on which TIGTA focused, its purpose was to ensure that managers had proper training to lead their employees and adapt to significant changes that were occurring at that time. The SB/SE Division comprises almost one-third of the total IRS work force and includes our largest enforcement staff, providing for the majority of the approximately $50 billion in annual enforcement revenue that the IRS collects. With the significant challenges facing the IRS, development of managers is critical to ensuring continued high performance across the IRS. At the time of this conference, almost 30 percent of SB/SE managers were either new to the division or new to management within the prior two years. Furthermore, SB/SE had grown by over 4,400 hires in FY 2009 and FY 2010 as a result of hiring initiatives approved by Congress. This division also faced unique challenges in FY 2010 and had to manage through significant employee concerns about safety and security after a member of the SB/SE management ranks was killed in a suicide attack against the IRS building in Austin, Texas. Employee safety and security training were important topics at the meeting with presentations by security personnel from TIGTA as well as the IRS.

Until late 2010, it was IRS practice to periodically conduct continuing professional education conferences on a national scale because of the importance and value of in-person training. However, in light of the continuing fiscal situation, improvements in technology, and recognizing the substantial costs of nationwide training meetings such as these, these types of meetings no longer occur. While the aggregate cost of the meeting is significant, it is important to note that the vast majority of the cost – more than 90 percent – resulted from travel and authorized government per diem for the attendees. Although the average cost per attendee was reasonable, the IRS recognizes that a number of less significant costs warranted additional scrutiny and were not the best use of government resources. Under subsequently issued guidance, many of these

3

expenditures, including promotional items or themed videos, would not be authorized. Cost savings guidance issued since this event include the following:

- December 14, 2010 – Deputy Commissioner – *Fiscal Year (FY) 2011 Hiring Freeze Guidance* – implementing exception-only hiring freeze
- February 9, 2011 – Commissioner – email to employees on cost-cutting
- February 10, 2011 – Chief Financial Officer – *FY 2011 Budget Operating Guidance* – working toward 50 percent reductions in non-mission critical travel, including management conferences
- February 28, 2011 – Deputy Commissioner – *FY 2011 Budget Operating Guidance Follow Up* – further restricting travel and training
- March 4, 2011 – Deputy Commissioner – *Workspace Budget Challenges* – reducing space holdings to cut cost
- August 19, 2011 – Deputy Commissioner – *Purchase of Promotional Items* – generally discontinuing purchase of any promotional items
- November 23, 2011 – Deputy Commissioner – *FY 2012 Budget Operating Guidance* – calling for further reductions in travel and training
- December 1, 2011 – Deputy Commissioner – *Approval of Conference-Related Activities* – implementing enhanced approval process for conference spending
- March 2, 2012 – Chief Financial Officer – *Interim Guidance Memorandum, Interim Guidance on Policies and Controls on Event-Related Spending* – implementing enhanced approval process for conference spending
- May 4, 2012 – Director, Office of Procurement Policy – *Acquiring Training, Meeting and Conference Space* – additional guidance for the selection of locations and facilities for IRS training activities
- May 8, 2012 – Deputy Commissioner – *Reinforcing Travel Policies and Updating Current Procedures* – reinforcing adherence to polices on travel expenditures
- May 29, 2012 – Deputy Commissioner – *Updating and Reinforcing Policies on Conferences, Group Conferences and Training* – reinforcing travel policies
- December 6, 2012 – Deputy Commissioner – *Fiscal Year 2013 Budget Operating Guidance* – further restricting travel and training
- December 27, 2012 – Chief Financial Officer – *Interim Guidance Memorandum, Reissued Interim Guidance on the Approval Process for Event-Related Spending* – implementing Treasury Directive 12-70, *Hosted or Sponsored Conference Planning and Approval*
- December 28, 2012 – Chief Financial Officer – *Guidance for Tracking Event-Related Spending* – implementing the requirement to track conference spending

4

- February 21, 2013 – Deputy Commissioner – *Servicewide Video Editorial Board* – creating a review board to oversee spending on video productions
- March 7, 2013 – Deputy Commissioner – *Additional Review on Video Production* – implementing mandatory high-level review on all video productions
- March 12, 2013 – Deputy Commissioner – *FY 2013 Budget Sequestration Operating Guidance* – increasing scrutiny and controls over hiring, travel, training, printing, contracts and overtime

It is also important to note that many of the issues raised in the report, such as the use of event planners, the receipt of room upgrades, and the welcome reception and breakfast provided by the hotel, did not entail the use of any additional government resources. While the IRS is mindful of the sensitivity of the issues raised, these did not impact the overall cost of the meeting. The IRS has instituted new procedures in these areas as well.

The IRS agrees with all of TIGTA's recommendations, and in most cases, has already implemented corrective actions in advance of receipt of the report. Our detailed comments to your recommendations are discussed in the attachment. If you have any questions, please contact me, or a member of your staff may contact Bill Maglin, Associate Chief Financial Officer for Financial Management, at (202) 435-5540.

Attachment

Attachment

RECOMMENDATION 1
The IRS Chief Financial Officer (CFO) should, for conferences held after issuance of the March 2012 procedures, verify that appropriate information is being tracked and maintained by IRS offices to accurately account for actual conference costs and attendance.

CORRECTIVE ACTION 1-1
The CFO issued the December 27, 2012 Interim Guidance Memorandum, *Reissued Interim Guidance on the Approval Process for Event-Related Spending*, requiring that documentation be maintained by the business units for conference and event-related spending. The CFO issued the December 28, 2012 memorandum, *Guidance for Tracking Event-Related Spending*, requiring that business units track actual costs and maintain documentation for conference and event-related spending.
RESPONSIBLE OFFICIAL
Chief Financial Officer
IMPLEMENTATION DATE
December 28, 2012 (Completed)

CORRECTIVE ACTION 1-2
The CFO will update the December 27, 2012 Interim Guidance Memorandum, *Reissued Interim Guidance on the Approval Process for Event-Related Spending*, to include a requirement for CFO to review on a rotating basis documentation maintained by the business units for conference and event-related spending.
RESPONSIBLE OFFICIAL
Chief Financial Officer
IMPLEMENTATION DATE
August 31, 2013

RECOMMENDATION 2
The IRS CFO should implement a policy to determine whether specific sessions at conferences qualify for CPE credit.

CORRECTIVE ACTION
The IRS Human Capital Office (HCO) will strengthen the policy and guidance for determining eligibility for course credit in IRM 6.410.1.2.6, *The Learning and Education Policy Manual*. The HCO will also strengthen the policy and guidance for determining when a course may be eligible for CPA CPE certification credit in IRM 6.410.1.3.3.3, *Credit for Continuing Professional Education for Certified Public Accountants*.
RESPONSIBLE OFFICIAL
Human Capital Office
IMPLEMENTATION DATE
August 31, 2013

2

RECOMMENDATION 3

The IRS CFO should reemphasize existing procedures to ensure business units contact Centralized Delivery Services (CDS) function personnel to coordinate planning of any future conference or event. Further, additional procedures should be developed that require all documentation supporting the selections of non-Government facilities for future conferences be maintained for management review.

CORRECTIVE ACTION 3-1

The HCO will update IRM 6.410.1, *Leadership and Education, Selection of Off-Site Locations and Facilities for Training*, to include procedures that require all documentation supporting the selection of non-Government facilities for future conferences be maintained for management review.
RESPONSIBLE OFFICIAL
Human Capital Office
IMPLEMENTATION DATE
October 1, 2013

CORRECTIVE ACTION 3-2

The Agency-Wide Shared Services (AWSS) Procurement office will update and reissue Policy and Procedures Memorandum No. 70.24, *Acquiring Training, Meeting and Conference Space*, to reflect guidance in Treasury Directive 12-70, *Hosted Conference/Special Event Planning*, to reemphasize existing procedures for planning conferences or events and maintaining supporting documentation.
RESPONSIBLE OFFICIAL
Agency-Wide Shared Services
IMPLEMENTATION DATE
August 31, 2013

RECOMMENDATION 4

The IRS CFO should develop and implement procedures outlining the appropriate use of outside event planners when planning IRS conferences. This should include how event planners are selected and compensated.

CORRECTIVE ACTION 4-1

The CFO issued the December 27, 2012 Interim Guidance Memorandum, *Reissued Interim Guidance on the Approval Process for Event-Related Spending*, which limits the use of external event planners.
RESPONSIBLE OFFICIAL
Chief Financial Officer
IMPLEMENTATION DATE
December 27, 2012 (Completed)

3

CORRECTIVE ACTION 4-2
The HCO will update IRM 6.410.1, *Leadership and Education, Selection of Off-Site Locations and Facilities for Training*, to include guidance on the use, selection and compensation if event planners must be used.
RESPONSIBLE OFFICIAL
Human Capital Office
IMPLEMENTATION DATE
October 1, 2013

RECOMMENDATION 5
The IRS CFO should establish procedures clearly outlining when planning trips should be performed for conferences. These procedures should require documentation of the reason and estimated cost for planning trips, along with the requirement that local IRS employees are used to the extent possible to perform these planning trips. This information should be provided to a designated management official or an executive for approval.

CORRECTIVE ACTION
The HCO will update IRM 6.410.1, *Leadership and Education, Selection of Off-Site Locations and Facilities for Training*, to emphasize the requirement to document the reason for and estimated cost of planning trips and to maintain documentation of executive approval of the planning trip.
RESPONSIBLE OFFICIAL
Human Capital Office
IMPLEMENTATION DATE
October 1, 2013

RECOMMENDATION 6
The IRS CFO should establish procedures to clearly outline the need for and value provided by any conference videos for future conferences. The purpose and use of videos should be clearly detailed in any request for a conference and include the applicable costs in the approval request.

CORRECTIVE ACTION
In February 2013, the IRS created the Servicewide Video Editorial Board (SVEB), which is chaired by the Communications and Liaison Communications Director and includes the Deputy Human Capital Officer and the Wage & Investment Communications Director. The SVEB reviews and approves all video projects planned throughout the IRS, considering cost, topic and tone, including training and education videos, webinars, vignettes, videos for external placement on YouTube, IRS.gov and related web sites, and any other ad hoc taping projects such as videos for use at IRS meetings and

4

conferences. A core part of the SVEB's efforts will be focused on ensuring that internal and external videos have a sound business purpose and advance tax administration interests, either through taxpayer education or internal training. The videos produced for the 2010 meeting would not be approved today under the SVEB's criteria. Mandatory higher level review is also currently in place.
RESPONSIBLE OFFICIAL
Communications and Liaison
IMPLEMENTATION DATE
February 21, 2013 (Completed)

RECOMMENDATION 7
The IRS CFO should evaluate whether the solicitation of hotel room suite upgrades for use by IRS employees should be allowed in agreements with hotels hosting IRS conferences in the future. In addition, any agreement with hotels containing hotel suite upgrades should be approved by the applicable business unit executive.

CORRECTIVE ACTION 7-1
The HCO will update IRM 6.410.1, *Leadership and Education, Selection of Off-Site Locations and Facilities for Training*, to prohibit the solicitation of room suite upgrades and where upgrades are offered at no cost to the IRS, require approval by the applicable business unit executive.
RESPONSIBLE OFFICIAL
Human Capital Office
IMPLEMENTATION DATE
October 1, 2013

CORRECTIVE ACTION 7-2
The AWSS Procurement office will update and reissue Policy and Procedures Memorandum No. 70.24, *Acquiring Training, Meeting and Conference Space*, to prohibit the solicitation of room suite upgrades and where upgrades are offered at no cost to the IRS, require approval by the applicable business unit executive.
RESPONSIBLE OFFICIAL
Agency-Wide Shared Services
IMPLEMENTATION DATE
August 31, 2013

RECOMMENDATION 8
The IRS CFO should identify all local employees who claimed per diem travel related to the conference and ensure Forms W-2 are issued to all employees for taxable travel as appropriate.

5

CORRECTIVE ACTION
The IRS will identify local employees who did not receive a Form W-2 for taxable travel and will issue them as appropriate.
RESPONSIBLE OFFICIAL
Chief Financial Officer
IMPLEMENTATION DATE
June 1, 2013

RECOMMENDATION 9
The IRS CFO should establish procedures to clearly outline the need for and value provided by any "information corridors"/exhibitor halls and other technology for future conferences. The purpose and use of any exhibitor hall or technology should be clearly detailed in any request for a conference and include the applicable costs, including giveaway items, in the approval request.

CORRECTIVE ACTION 9-1
The CFO issued the December 27, 2012 Interim Guidance Memorandum, *Reissued Interim Guidance on the Approval Process for Event-Related Spending*, which outlines the requirements to include the full-cost of events when submitting events for approval.
RESPONSIBLE OFFICIAL
Chief Financial Officer
IMPLEMENTATION DATE
December 27, 2012 (Completed)

CORRECTIVE ACTION 9-2
The HCO will update IRM 6.410.1, *Leadership and Education, Selection of Off-Site Locations and Facilities for Training*, to reflect guidance on the analysis of the use of exhibitor halls and specialized technology.
RESPONSIBLE OFFICIAL
Human Capital Office
IMPLEMENTATION DATE
October 1, 2013